200 ten-minute meals

hamlyn | all color cookbook

200 ten-minute meals

Denise Smart

An Hachette UK Company
www.hachette.co.uk

First published in Great Britain in 2013 by Hamlyn
a division of Octopus Publishing Group Ltd
Endeavour House, 189 Shaftesbury Avenue
London WC2H 8JY
www.octopusbooksusa.com

Distributed in the US by
Hachette Book Group USA
237 Park Avenue
New York NY 10017 USA

Distributed in Canada by
Canadian Manda Group
165 Dufferin Street
Toronto, Ontario, Canada M6K 3H6

ISBN: 978-0-600-62617-6

Printed and bound in China

10 9 8 7 6 5 4 3 2 1

Standard level spoon and cup measurements
are used in all recipes.

Ovens should be preheated to the specified temperature—
if using a convection oven, follow the manufacturer's
instructions for adjusting the time and temperature.

Fresh herbs should be used unless otherwise stated.
Large eggs should be used unless otherwise stated.

This book includes dishes made with nuts and nut
derivatives. It is advisable for those with known allergic
reactions to nuts and nut derivatives to avoid dishes made
with these. It is prudent to check the labels of all prepared
ingredients for the possible inclusion of nut derivatives.
Vulnerable people, such as pregnant and nursing
mothers, people with weakened immune systems, the
elderly, babies, and young children, should avoid dishes
containing raw or lightlly cooked eggs.

Some of the recipes in this book have previously appeared
in other titles published by Hamlyn.

contents

introduction

introduction

Can you really cook a delicious meal in only 10 minutes? Yes, you can! All it takes is some planning ahead, a well-stocked refrigerator, freezer, and pantry, and a little help from your supermarket, fish dealer, and butcher.

In the time it would take you to pick up the telephone and order a takeout meal, or prick the plastic film on a prepared meal and wait for it to heat up in the microwave, you could have made a much more delicious and nutritious dinner from scratch.

If you've had a long day, the car broke down, the train was delayed, you've been stuck in traffic trying to get home or had to work late, the last thing you want to do

is think about planning, shopping for, and cooking a meal. However, follow these few simple guidelines and you will be able to put together a tasty, wholesome meal in a matter of minutes.

Take a little time out and do a weekly meal plan so you know what you are going to cook and can organize your shopping accordingly, thus making sure you have everything on hand and can avoid waste. Why not make use of Internet shopping? After doing this the first time, subsequent grocery orders becomes quicker and easier as you build up your shopping profile and get used to the system. The food is delivered to you at your convenience. This alone could save you hours each month.

ingredients

To make food taste delicious in double-quick time, you will need to add plenty of flavorsome ingredients that will have an instant impact on your dish, so make sure to stock up on your favorite purees, herbs, spices, and sauces.

You can also try keeping flowerpots of herbs growing on your windowsill—apart from looking attractive, they will make sure you have a supply of fresh herbs on hand that will liven up a variety of recipes. Just remember to water them from time to time!

Jars of already chopped or minced ginger, garlic, and lemon grass are great time-savers and will make a huge reduction

in your preparation time. You can buy meat and fish already trimmed and cut into chunks or strips. Not only will you save on the preparation time, but these small pieces cook quickly, too. Many vegetables can also be purchased already peeled and chopped, again saving valuable minutes in the kitchen at the end of a long, busy day.

Cooking a meal in just 10 minutes inevitably involves the clever use of prepared ingredients. You can find all the items that are used in these recipes in major supermarkets. Below is a list of the more commonly used ingredients in this book, ingredients that will be helpful to keep on hand in your pantry, refrigerator, and freezer.

the pantry

The most useful source of quick meals is probably the pantry, or a cupboard or two. After reading through the recipes in this book, you will soon be able to create some quick culinary masterpieces of your own, even if you haven't organized or planned to cook a specific dish.

Remember to keep a list of the items you have used, so you can restock next time you go shopping. Organize your pantry so that things are always easy to find, and remember that once some items, such as jars of purees or packages of coconut milk, are opened, they need to be stored in the refrigerator to keep them fresh.

pantry essentials
canned foods
- diced tomatoes
- legumes, such as chickpeas, kidney beans, lentils, and lima beans
- vegetables and fruit, such as corn kernels and pineapple
- fish, such as salmon and tuna, in oil or water, as well as anchovy fillets
- coconut milk

jars
- tomato paste and ketchup
- Worcestershire sauce
- curry pastes and harissa
- sweet chili sauce
- dark soy sauce
- English, French, and whole-grain mustards
- Thai fish sauce
- wasabi paste
- mango chutney and caramelized onions
- a selection of oils, such as sunflower, olive, and sesame oil
- a selection of vinegars, such as balsamic and white wine vinegar

sweet things
- honey and maple syrup
- prepared fruit sauces and chocolate sauce
- extracts, such as vanilla, peppermint, and orange
- granulated sugar and brown sugar
- prepared piecrusts and meringues

herbs, spices & flavorings
- chopped or minced garlic, ginger, and lemon grass
- dried herbs, such as thyme and mint
- spices, such as Cajun seasoning, chili powder, paprika, cinnamon, and curry powder
- salt and black pepper
- good-quality bouillon cubes
- good-quality gravy granules

dry ingredients
- all-purpose flour
- cornstrach
- quick-cooking types of dried pasta, such as angel hair and orzo
- couscous
- instant rice, vacuum-packed in envelopes
- already cooked stir-fry noodles
- chopped cashew nuts, peanuts, and pecans
- sesame seeds

the refrigerator

Fresh produce, such as meat, fish, and seafood, should be bought as fresh as possible and with specific meals in mind to reduce wastage. If timing allows, it's best to buy them on the day you're planning to cook them if you can.

It is also a good idea to get to know your local butcher and fish dealer; this way you can get them to do a lot of the preparation for you, saving you time in the kitchen later. Otherwise make use of the butchers and fish dealers to be found in the larger supermarkets.

refrigerator essentials
- bags of prepared salad greens, such as arugula, mixed lettuce, and baby spinach
- packages of chopped stir-fry vegetables and bean sprouts
- packages of chopped onions and sliced mushrooms
- fresh vegetables, such as red bell peppers, new potatoes, scallions, and carrots
- diced or chopped pancetta and chorizo
- sliced cooked meats, such as chicken, and ham
- fresh bread crumbs
- fresh pasta and gnocchi
- prepared mashed potatoes
- grated Parmesan and cheddar cheese
- yogurt, such as Greek and plain
- butter
- eggs
- heavy cream, crème fraîche (optional), and sour cream
- containers of fresh cheese sauce, tomato sauce, and pesto
- containers of prepared fresh tomato salsa and guacamole

the freezer

This is a much underused kitchen appliance nowadays, but the freezer is not only essential for storing foods that are bought frozen but also for storing foods that you prepare and freeze yourself.

Frozen food is frequently thought of as inferior to fresh produce, but the opposite is often true: frozen vegetables, such as peas, contain more vitamins than fresh ones because they are frozen just after picking, when they are at their very best. Freezing also allows you to enjoy your favorite fruits and vegetables whenever you like, whether they are in season or not.

Frozen meat is not only just as nutritious as fresh, but it is often cheaper. In many ways, frozen fish and seafood are even better than fresh: when fish is frozen at sea as soon as it is caught, all the taste and goodness is locked in. And it is often better for the environment, too, because frozen fish does not have to be air-freighted but can be transported by ship or overland.

For the best results, thaw frozen seafood or meat by placing it in the refrigerator overnight. Once it has thawed, do not refreeze it, otherwise treat it as you would fresh produce.

Frozen food will, of course, also keep for much longer than fresh, and you can reduce food waste by freezing it in portions and only thawing and using the amount you need for each meal. Bread keeps well in the freezer, so freeze pita bread, naan, and halved English muffins or bagels so you always have a useful supply on hand.

If you are organized enough and have a few minutes to spare, you can make your own bread crumbs from slightly stale bread—the food processor makes light work of this task—and freeze them for use later.

You can also freeze your own grated ginger and chopped garlic, or grate some cheddar and Parmesan cheese and freeze it in small containers for meals later in the week.

When cooking rice as an accompaniment, cook extra quantities to freeze in portions. Try cooking a double quantity of some dishes, such as Creamy Paprika Chicken (see page 124) or Thai Massaman Chicken Curry (see page 114), so you can freeze half to create a quick, microwavable meal.

- bread, such as naan, pita, and sliced white
- ice cream
- bags of berries, such as raspberries, blueberries, and mixed berries
- squid rings and shrimp (remember to defrost them in the refrigerator)
- ready-to-bake puff pastry

equipment

Do not underestimate how vitally important good tools are to speed up the cooking process. To prepare a quick and simple meal, all you need are a few good-quality items of kitchen equipment.

- A large, heavy skillet or wok. This is essential for many of the quick-to-cook recipes in this book. A thick, heavy bottom spreads the heat evenly, letting you cook at high temperatures without burning. An ovenproof or detachable handle is a useful feature so you can continue cooking under the broiler or in the oven.
- A selection of good-quality saucepans with lids, a ridged grill pan, a large colander, and a strainer are also essential.
- Good knives are vital. You will need at least two: a small knife for paring and slicing, and a larger one for chopping. Remember that a sharp knife will enable you to work more quickly and is safer than a blunt one.
- Basic utensils, such as spoons for stirring, a spatula, a slotted spoon, vegetable peeler, wire whisk, and a pair of tongs are also needed.

freezer essentials
- bags of mixed vegetables, such as Mediterranean vegetables
- bags of peas
- containers of chopped chile, garlic, and ginger, and herbs, such as parsley and cilantro

14

- A grater is another invaluable tool. Choose one that is comfortable to hold, has a range of different blades, and is sharp. Microplanes are fantastic for quickly removing the rind from citrus fruits.
- Make sure you have at least two baking sheets and a selection of bowls of different sizes for mixing.
- Don't forget a set of measuring spoons and cups plus a liquid measuring cup for measuring ingredients.
- You will also need at least two cutting boards, so that you can keep one for preparing vegetables and fruit and a separate board for meat and fish.

electric appliances
Some electrical equipment can also help you save time. Buy a good-quality food processor to make quick work of whipping up pastes and pestos, blending soups, and chopping fruits and nuts. An electric handheld mixer is another great time-saving device, letting you quickly beat eggs and cream without much effort. Finally, a microwave has many uses apart from reheating ready meals. Use it to melt chocolate, defrost frozen foods, reheat prepared mashed potatoes, and cook vegetables to serve with some of your 10-minute meals.

quick-cooking methods

Most recipes in this book use one of the following quick-cooking methods. Follow the tips below for guaranteed success.
Stir-frying You will need a wok or a large, deep skillet. Preheat the wok or skillet until hot, then add the oil. Make sure the oil is very hot before adding the ingredients, because this will ensure the food is sealed quickly on the outside to retain all its juices and browns to develop maximum flavor. Cut meat and vegetables into even pieces so they all cook at the same rate.
Deep-frying You can use a wok or deep saucepan if you don't have a deep fryer.

Make sure the oil is hot enough before adding the food. Use a thermometer to check the temperature or drop a cube of bread into the oil; when the bread turns golden in 15 seconds, the oil has reached the correct temperature. If the temperature of the oil is too low, the food will be soggy and absorb a lot of oil. If you are using a deep fryer, you can set the dial to the correct temperature.

Broiling Make sure the broiler is preheated to high before placing the food under it. Place the food as near to the heat as possible, without it touching.

Grilling When grilling, lightly oil the food on both sides before adding it to the pan. Preheat the grill pan until very hot before

adding the food. If you need to oil the pan, dip a piece of paper towel in a little oil, rub it over the surface of the pan, preheat the pan, and when it is smoking, add the food.

tips for organizing your kitchen

Make your kitchen works for you, so you can find things quickly. Next time you have a spare hour, reorganize your kitchen to make it easier to work in.

- It may sound obvious, but place frequently used utensils, such as wooden spoons, tongs, and spatulas, next to the oven in a pitcher or jar, or hanging from a rail, so they are close by when you need them.
- Reorganize your cutlery and utensils drawer so that items you use most are at

the front. Keep knives in a knife block or rack on top of the countertop, not stuck at the back of a drawer, where they will become blunt and will probably cut you.

- Don't hide the food processor and handheld mixer at the back of a cabinet or behind heavy equipment so they are hard to reach and too much of an effort to use.
- Keep mixing bowls and measuring equipment together, baking sheets in a drawer near the oven, and ovenproof dishes in an easy-to-reach place.
- Keep your work surface free from clutter, so you have plenty of space to work. A tidy kitchen will make you feel more organized and this, in turn, will help you to work faster and more efficiently.

complete your meal

It may be fine to cook a recipe in a matter of minutes, but how do you turn that into a well-balanced and satisfying meal? If a dish can be cooked in 10 minutes, you don't want to spend any more time than necessary making an accompaniment to serve with it.

Prepared mashed potatoes bought from the refrigerated section in the supermarket and packages of precooked stir-fry noodles and instant rice make great accompaniments to a variety of dishes—and take just a few minutes to prepare. And don't forget bread as a nutritious, satisfying and quick accompaniment, from soft, fresh bread or rolls to crusty bread with a bowl of soup, stew, or other main dish. However, if a dish already contains a carbohydrate, such as rice, pasta, or potatoes, serve it with some green salad or an additional portion of vegetables instead.

Frozen vegetables, such as frozen spinach and peas, are quick to cook, especially in the microwave. Most supermarkets stock a good range of prepared fresh vegetables, such as snow peas, sugar snaps, asparagus, and green beans, which take a matter of minutes to cook in a saucepan of salted boiling water

while you are cooking your main dish. And prepared salad greens, tomatoes, cucumber, and other raw ingredients are quickly assembled into a vitamin-packed salad.

how to follow the recipes

- Before you start cooking, make sure you have all the ingredients on hand as well as the right cooking utensils and equipment.
- Always first read all the way through the recipe, so you know what will happen ahead. You may need to preheat a broiler or oven, or heat oil in a wok or deep fryer.
- You will need to learn the art of multitasking; while something is cooking in one pan, you may need to be stirring something else in another pan. Once you've done this a few times, you will find it gets easier and you will get quicker!
- Take the recipes one step at a time, following the steps in order. You will need to prepare or chop the next ingredients as you work, while you are waiting for other ingredients to cook, instead of doing all the preparation at the beginning, to complete the recipes in 10 minutes.
- Make sure the stock is hot by dissolving bouillon cubes in boiling water. Invest in an electric kettle—using boiling water from it to fill a saucepan for cooking vegetables, pasta, and rice will help keep the cooking times within 10 minutes.
- While you are cooking, get other members of the household to lay the table for you.

Getting children involved in some stage of the procedure, whether it is helping to stir the food or laying the table, will encourage happy mealtimes.

- Don't get stressed! It will slow you down and ruin what should be an enjoyable experience. If a recipe takes 12 minutes instead of 10, don't worry. We all work at different rates and some people will be able to chop quicker than others.
- Finally, have fun: Enjoy the aromas and the success of a quick and delicious meal coming together.

snacks &
light meals

tuna quesadilla with salsa

Serves **2**
Preparation time **4 minutes**
Cooking time **4–6 minutes**

2 **soft flour tortillas**
¼ cup **prepared fresh
  tomato salsa**
2 **scallions**, coarsely chopped
1 (5 oz) **can tuna**, drained
⅓ cup **canned corn kernels
  with red bell peppers**,
  drained
½ cup shredded
  mozzarella cheese
olive oil, for brushing

Place 1 tortilla on a plate and spread with the salsa.
Sprinkle with the scallions, tuna, corn kernels, and
cheese. Place the second tortilla on top and press down.

Heat a large skillet and brush with oil. Place the
quesadilla in the skillet and cook over moderate heat
for 2–3 minutes, pressing down with a spatula until the
cheese starts to melt.

Place an inverted plate over the skillet and turn the
skillet and plate together to transfer the quesadilla onto
the plate. Slide back into the skillet and cook the other
side for 2–3 minutes. Remove from the skillet and cut
into wedges.

For prosciutto tortilla pizzas, place 2 soft flour
tortillas on a large baking sheet and spread with
¼ cup prepared pizza sauce. Arrange 4 chopped slices
of proscuitto and 4 oz sliced mozzarella on top. Cook
under a preheated hot broiler for 2–3 minutes, until
the cheese has melted. Serve immediately with a large
handful of arugula leaves sprinkled over the top and a
drizzle of olive oil.

Muenster, orange & mint salad

Serves **2**
Preparation time **6 minutes**
Cooking time **2–4 minutes**

2 **oranges,** peeled
¼ cup **chopped mint**
2 teaspoons **white wine vinegar**
2 tablespoons **olive oil**
1 teaspoon **honey**
⅓ cup **pine nuts**
8 oz **Muenster cheese,** cut into 8–10 slices
1 (5 oz) package **prepared baby spinach salad**
salt and **black pepper**

Divide the oranges into segments by cutting between the membranes, working over a bowl to catch the juice. Whisk the mint, vinegar, olive oil, and honey into the juice and season to taste.

Heat a skillet until hot, add the pine nuts, and dry-fry for 1–2 minutes, stirring occasionally, until golden.

Meanwhile, heat a ridged grill pan until hot. Grill the cheese slices for 1–2 minutes on each side, until golden.

Divide the leaves and orange segments between 2 serving bowls, arrange the cheese on top, and sprinkle with the pine nuts. Spoon the dressing over the topand serve immediately.

For Muenster with lemon & caper dressing, place 2 tablespoons olive oil in a bowl with the finely grated rind and juice of 1 small lemon, 1 tablespoon white wine vinegar, 1 teaspoon Dijon mustard, 2 tablespoons chopped parsley, and 1 tablespoon capers. Season to taste and whisk together. Cut 8 oz Muenster cheese into 8 slices and heat a ridged grill pan until hot. Cook the cheese for 1–2 minutes on each side, until golden. Divide the cheese between 2 plates, drizzle with the dressing, and serve immediately with warmed pita breads.

shrimp & rice paper wraps

Serves **2**
Preparation time **10 minutes**

3 **dried rice paper wrappers**
   (banh trang), **8** inches
   in diameter
½ **small carrot**, cut into thin
   strips
2 **Chinese cabbage leaves**,
   shredded
¼ cup **bean sprouts**
¼ cup **chopped fresh cilantro**
4 oz **cooked, peeled**
   jumbo shrimp
1 tablespoon **Thai fish sauce**
6 **mint leaves**
sweet chili dipping sauce,
   to serve

Place one of the wrappers in a bowl of warm water until softened and opaque. Shake off the excess water and lay on a plate.

Place the carrot, Chinese cabbage, bean sprouts, cilantro, and shrimp in a bowl and mix well.

Brush the middle of the wrapper with fish sauce, lay 2 mint leaves on it, then place one-third of the shrimp mixture in a line down the middle. Fold in both sides of the wrapper, then roll up tightly.

Cover with a damp cloth and repeat with the remaining wrappers and filling. Cut each roll in half and serve immediately with the dipping sauce.

For shrimp & lettuce cups, mix 8 oz cooked, peeled shrimp with ¾ cup peeled and diced mango, ½ cup bean sprouts, and 2 tablespoons chopped fresh cilantro. Arrange 8 outer leaves of Boston lettuce on a plate, rounded sides down. Fill the leaves with the shrimp mixture and drizzle with a little sweet chili dipping sauce. Serve immediately.

balsamic figs with prosciutto

Serves **4**
Preparation time **5 minutes**
Cooking time **4–5 minutes**

8 **ripe figs**, halved
2 tablespoons
    balsamic vinegar
extra virgin olive oil, for
    drizzling
12 slices of **prosciutto**
2 cups **arugula**
salt and **black pepper**

Arrange the fig halves, cut side up, on a baking sheet.
Brush with the vinegar and lightly drizzle with oil.
Season with a little salt and a generous grinding of
black pepper.

Cook under a preheated hot broiler for 4–5 minutes,
until heated through and a little charred.

Arrange 3 slices of prosciutto on each serving plate.
Top with the grilled figs and sprinkle with arugula.
Drizzle with a little more oil and serve while the figs
are still warm.

For minted melon with prosciutto, peel and slice a
small, ripe melon and arrange on a platter with 12 slices
of prosciutto. Sprinkle with 5 mint leaves, coarsely torn,
and drizzle with extra virgin olive oil.

croque monsieur

Serves **2**
Preparation time **4 minutes**
Cooking time **6 minutes**

4 slices of **crusty white bread**
1 tablespoon **Dijon mustard**
2 thick slices of **ham**
4 slices of **Gruyère** or
  Swiss cheese
1 extra-large **egg**
2 tablespoons **milk**
1 tablespoon **sunflower oil**
salt and **black pepper**

Spread 2 slices of the bread with the mustard, then top each with a slice of ham and 2 slices of cheese. Place the remaining bread on top to make 2 sandwiches.

Beat together the egg and milk in a shallow dish and season to taste. Heat the oil in a large, nonstick skillet.

Place the sandwiches in the egg mixture, let sit for 1 minute, then turn over and let sit for another minute.

Cook the sandwiches in the skillet for 3 minutes on each side, until golden brown and the cheese has melted. Serve immediately.

For onion & cheese toasts, place 2 thick slices of white bread under a preheated hot broiler and toast lightly on both sides. Spread each slice with 1 tablespoon onion relish, and divide 1 cup shredded Gruyère or Swiss cheese between them. Return to the broiler and cook for 2–3 minutes, until the cheese is bubbling and golden. Serve immediately with a crisp green salad.

chicken caesar salad

Serves **4**
Preparation time **7–8 minutes**

2 **Romaine lettuce**
1 **ripe avocado**, peeled,
   pitted, and chopped
12 oz **prepared chicken
   slices**
1¾ cups **croutons**

Dressing
⅓ cup **low-fat crème fraîche**
   or **sour cream**
2 **anchovy fillets in oil**,
   drained
¼ cup grated **Parmesan
   cheese**, plus extra to serve
finely grated rind and juice of
   ½ **lemon**
freshly ground black pepper

Place the crème fraîche or sour cream in a food
processor with the anchovy fillets, Parmesan, and lemon
rind and juice. Blend to make a smooth dressing and
season to taste with black pepper.

Tear the lettuce into bite-size pieces and place in a
bowl with the avocado. Pour the dressing over the top,
toss together, and divide among 4 bowls.

Arrange the chicken on top and sprinkle with the
croutons. Season with black pepper and sprinkle with
a little Parmesan. Serve immediately.

For warm salmon Caesar salad, cut 4 skinless
salmon fillets, about 5 oz each, lengthwise into 4 strips.
Lightly oil a ridged grill pan and heat over medium heat.
Cook the salmon strips for 1–2 minutes on each side,
until just cooked. Meanwhile, prepare the dressing and
salad as above, omitting the chicken. Divide the salad
among 4 bowls and top with the salmon. Season with
black pepper and sprinkle with a little grated Parmesan.

crab cocktail with baby avocados

Serves **4**
Preparation time **10 minutes**

¼ cup **mayonnaise**
2 tablespoons **Greek yogurt**
3 tablespoons **lime juice**
½–1 teaspoon **wasabi paste**
2 tablespoons **chopped fresh cilantro**
8 oz **fresh, prepared white crabmeat**
4 ripe **baby avocados**
salt and **black pepper**
prepared salad greens, to garnish

Mix together the mayonnaise and yogurt, then stir in 1 tablespoon of the lime juice and the wasabi paste to taste. Add the cilantro and crabmeat, season to taste, and toss to mix well.

Cut the avocados in half lengthwise and remove the pits, then brush with the remaining lime juice. Place 2 halves on each serving plate.

Fill the avocados with the crab mixture and garnish with salad greens. Serve immediately.

For shrimp cocktail with lime & cilantro mayonnaise, separate the leaves from 3 Boston lettuce and divide among 4 glasses. Mix ⅓ cup mayonnaise with 1 tablespoon lime juice, 2 drops of Tabasco sauce, and 2 tablespoons chopped fresh cilantro. Stir in 1 lb cooked, peeled shrimp, then spoon the mixture over the lettuce. Serve immediately with lime wedges for squeezing.

lima bean & anchovy pâté

Serves **2–3**
Preparation time **8 minutes**

1 (15 oz) **can lima beans**,
    drained and rinsed
1 (2 oz) **can anchovy fillets
    in oil**, drained
2 **scallions**, finely chopped
2 tablespoons **lemon juice**
1 tablespoon **olive oil**
¼ cup **chopped fresh cilantro**
black pepper
4–6 slices of **rye bread**,
    toasted, to serve

Place all the ingredients, except the cilantro, in a food processor and blend until well mixed but still coarse in texture. Alternatively, mash the beans with a fork, finely chop the anchovies, and mix the ingredients together by hand.

Stir in the cilantro and season well with black pepper. Serve with toasted rye bread.

For lima bean & mushroom pâté, cook 3 cups sliced mushrooms in 2 tablespoons olive oil with 1 finely chopped garlic clove until the mushrooms are tender and all the liquid has evaporated. Let cool, then follow the main recipe, using the mushrooms instead of the anchovies.

quail eggs with prosciutto

Serves **2**
Preparation time **3 minutes**
Cooking time **6 minutes**

¼ cup **prepared**
  hollandaise sauce
1 teaspoon **Dijon mustard**
2 slices of **prosciutto**
2 **English muffins**, split
2 tablespoons **butter**,
  softened
4 **quail eggs**
salad greens, to serve
  (optional)

Mix the hollandaise sauce with the mustard and set aside. Heat a small skillet until hot, add the prosciutto, and dry-fry for 1–2 minutes on each side, until crispy. Meanwhile, toast the muffins, spread with some of the butter, and keep warm.

Brush a nonstick skillet with the remaining butter and place over moderate heat until hot. Break in the eggs and cook for 2 minutes.

Divide the muffin halves between 2 plates, arrange the eggs on top, and spoon the sauce over the top. Serve immediately with the crisp ham and salad greens, if desired.

For quail eggs with asparagus, cook 8 oz trimmed asparagus spears in a large saucepan of lightly salted boiling water for 3–4 minutes, until just tender. Drain and keep warm. Meanwhile, place 4 quail eggs in a small saucepan of cold water and bring to a boil, remove from the heat, and let stand for 30 seconds. Peel and cut each egg in half. Prepare the mustard hollandaise as above. Divide the asparagus and eggs between 2 plates, spoon the hollandaise over the top, and serve immediately with crusty bread.

greek feta & mint dip

Serves **4**
Preparation time **5 minutes**
Cooking time **2–4 minutes**

1 cup **feta cheese**
½ **small red onion**,
  thinly sliced
handful of **mint leaves**,
  finely chopped
1 cup **Greek yogurt**
8 whole-wheat **pita breads**
freshly ground black pepper
sliced ripce black olives,
  to garnish

Mix the cheese with the onion, mint, and yogurt, season with black pepper, and stir gently to combine. Transfer to a serving bowl and sprinkle with a few sliced olives.

Cook the pita breads under a preheated hot broiler for 1–2 minutes each side, until lightly toasted. Cut into strips and serve with the dip.

For Greek feta pita pockets, toast 4 pita breads and slice open. Meanwhile, mix 12 halved cherry tomatoes with ½ small chopped cucumber, a small handful of sliced ripe black olives, and 1 ⅓ cups crumbled feta cheese. Whisk 2 tablespoons olive oil with 2 teaspoons red wine vinegar and a large pinch of dried oregano and season to taste. Pour the daressing over the salad ingredients and mix well. Place some shredded lettuce in each pita bread and spoon in the Greek salad mixture. Serve immediately.

Muenster with paprika oil

Serves **4**
Preparation time **5 minutes**
Cooking time **5 minutes**

⅓ cup **extra virgin olive oil**
¼ cup **lemon juice**
½ teaspoon **smoked paprika**
8 oz **Muenster cheese**, cut
   into chunks
salt and **black pepper**

Combine the oil, lemon juice, and paprika in a small bowl and season the mixture with salt and black pepper.

Heat a heavy skillet until hot, then add the Muenster and toss over medium heat until golden and starting to soften. Transfer immediately to a plate, drizzle with the paprika oil, and serve with toothpicks to spike the cheese.

lentil & goat cheese salad

Serves **4**
Preparation time **10 minutes**

1 (5 oz) package **baby spinach**
1 (15 oz) can **lentils in water**, drained and rinsed
¾ cup drained and chopped **roasted red peppers from a jar**
½ cup **walnut pieces**
4 oz **fresh goat cheese**, coarsely crumbled

Dressing
2 tablespoons **balsamic vinegar**
3 tablespoons **walnut oil**
1 teaspoon **Dijon mustard**
salt and **black pepper**

Place the spinach, lentils, roasted peppers, and walnut pieces in a bowl and mix gently.

Whisk together the dressing ingredients in a small bowl and season to taste. Pour the dressing over the lentil mixture and toss lightly to combine. Divide among 4 bowls and top with the cheese.

For beet & goat cheese salad, cut 8 cooked beets into wedges and place in a bowl with ⅓ cup toasted pine nuts and 1 (5 oz) package mixed salad greens. Whisk 1 tablespoon balsamic vinegar with 2 tablespoons olive oil and 2 teaspoons honey and season to taste. Pour the dressing over the salad and gently toss together. Divide among 4 plates and top with 7 oz crumbled goat cheese. Serve immediately.

naan pizzas

Serves **4**
Preparation time **2 minutes**
Cooking time **6–8 minutes**

2 **plain naans** or **bagels**,
  halved
¼ cup **mango chutney**
4 oz **cooked tandoori**
  chicken or **other**
  seasoned chicken,
  chopped (about 1 cup)
½ **small red bell pepper**,
  cored, seeded, and sliced
1 cup shredded **mozzarella**
  cheese
2 tablespoons **chopped**
  fresh cilantro
Greek yogurt, to serve
  (optional)

Preheat the oven to 400°F. Place the naans or halved bagels on a large baking sheet and spread with the mango chutney.

Arrange the chopped chicken and bell peppers on top and sprinkle with the cheese. Bake in the preheated oven for 6–8 minutes, until bubbling and golden.

Sprinkle with the cilantro, cut in half, and serve immediately with Greek yogurt, if desired.

For ciabatta pizzas, split a ciabatta loaf in half lengthwise. Cook under a preheated hot broiler for 2 minutes on each side. Spread each cut side with 3 tablespoons tomato paste, and then divide 4 oz sliced mozzarella and 7 halved cherry tomatoes between the pizzas. Cook under a preheated hot broiler for 3–4 minutes, until the cheese has melted. Cut the pizzas in half and serve immediately sprinkled with basil leaves.

tomato, hot pepper & tofu salad

Serves **2**
Preparation time **8 minutes**
Cooking time **1–2 minutes**

3 tablespoons **pine nuts**
1 **large beefsteak tomato**,
   thinly sliced
4 oz **tofu**
¼ cup drained and thinly
   sliced **hot piquante**
   peppers from a jar
3 tablespoons **snipped chives**
2 tablespoons **chopped**
   flat-leaf parsley
¼ cup **golden raisins**
¼ cup **olive oil**
2 tablespoons **lemon juice**
2 teaspoons **granulated**
   sugar
salt and **black pepper**
crusty bread, to serve

Heat a skillet until hot, add the pine nuts, and dry-fry for 1–2 minutes, stirring occasionally, until golden.

Arrange the tomato slices on 2 serving plates and season lightly. Crumble the tofu into a mixing bowl, add the piquante peppers, chives, parsley, pine nuts, and golden raisins, and mix together.

Whisk the olive oil with the lemon juice and sugar, season to taste, and toss with the tofu mixture. Spoon the dressing over the tomatoes and serve with crusty bread.

For spinach & tofu salad, crumble the tofu into a mixing bowl, add the herbs, pine nuts, golden raisins, and 3 tablespoons lime juice. Heat 2 teaspoons peanut oil in a large skillet. Add 1 crushed garlic clove, cook for a few seconds, then add 1 (6 oz) package baby spinach. Cook until wilted, then toss with the tofu salad and serve with crusty bread.

thai chile chicken strips

Serves **4**
Preparation time **5 minutes**
Cooking time **5 minutes**

oil, for brushing
12 oz **boneless, skinless chicken breast tenderloins**
lime wedges, to serve

Sauce
2 teaspoons **brown sugar**
1 tablespoon **prepared chopped ginger**
1 teaspoon **lemon grass paste**
3 tablespoons **sweet chili sauce**
2 tablespoons **rice wine vinegar**
finely grated rind and juice of **1 lime**
¼ cup **dark soy sauce**

Brush a ridged grill pan with a little oil and heat over high heat until hot. Meanwhile, cut each chicken tenderloin in half lengthwise. Mix together all the sauce ingredients in a bowl, add the strips of chicken, and mix well.

Cook the chicken strips in the hot pan for 3 minutes, brushing with any remaining sauce. Turn over and cook for an additional 2 minutes. Serve immediately with lime wedges.

For Thai chicken soup, heat 1 tablespoon oil in a medium saucepan and add 2 tablespoons Thai red or green curry paste. Cook for 1 minute, then stir in 1 teaspoon lemon grass paste, 3½ cups coconut milk, and 1 tablespoon Thai fish sauce. Bring to a boil, reduce the heat, stir in 1 cup drained, canned bamboo shoots, and simmer for 2–3 minutes. Meanwhile, coarsely shred 12 oz cooked chicken breast (about 2 cups) and stir into the soup with 2 tablespoons chopped fresh cilantro. Simmer for 2 minutes, until the chicken is heated through. Add 3 tablespoons lime juice and serve immediately.

salt & pepper squid

Serves **2**
Preparation time **2 minutes**
Cooking time **6 minutes**

⅓ cup **sunflower oil**
¼ cup **cornstarch**
½ teaspoon **salt**
1 teaspoon **freshly ground
  black pepper**
½ teaspoon **Chinese five
  spice powder**
8 oz **raw squid rings**
lemon wedges, to serve

Heat the oil in a deep fryer or deep, heavy saucepan to 350°F, or until a cube of bread browns in 15 seconds.

Place the cornstarch, salt, black pepper, and five spice in a large bowl and mix together. Add the squid and toss in the mixture to coat the rings evenly. Shake off any excess.

Cook half the squid in the hot oil for 2 minutes, then turn and cook for an additional minute, until lightly golden. Remove with a slotted spoon and drain on paper towels. Repeat with the remaining squid. Serve immediately with lemon wedges.

For pan-fried squid with garlic, parsley & bread crumbs, heat 1 tablespoon olive oil in a skillet and add 1 teaspoon prepared chopped garlic. Cook for 1–2 minutes, until lightly golden. Stir in 8 oz raw squid rings and stir to coat in the oil. Add ½ cup fresh white bread crumbs and cook, stirring from time to time, for 3–4 minutes, until the crumbs are crisp and the squid is just cooked. Stir in 1 tablespoon chopped parsley and season to taste. Remove the skillet from the heat and squeeze 2 tablespoons lemon juice over the squid. Stir well and serve immediately.

chilled avocado soup

Serves **4**
Preparation time **10 minutes**

3 **ripe avocados**, peeled,
    pitted, and diced
1 **small red onion**, coarsely
    chopped
3–4 drops **Tabasco sauce**
3 tablespoons **lime juice**
2½ cups **buttermilk**
¼ cup **chopped fresh cilantro**
12 **ice cubes**
soft flour tortillas, warmed
    and cut into strips, to serve

Place the avocado in a food processor, reserving a handful for garnish, with all the remaining ingredients except the ice cubes and blend until smooth.

Divide among 4 glass bowls and top each portion with 3 ice cubes and some of the reserved avocado. Serve immediately with warmed tortilla strips

For avocado & bacon salad, cook 8 smoked bacon slices under a preheated hot broiler for 3–4 minutes on each side, until crispy, then drain on paper towels. Meanwhile, mix ¼ cup mayonnaise with 1 teaspoon whole-grain mustard and 2 tablespoons white wine vinegar. Peel, pit, and slice 2 ripe avocados and place in a salad bowl with 1 (12 oz) package baby spinach and 12 halved cherry tomatoes. Cut the bacon into pieces and add to the salad with the dressing. Toss gently together and serve immediately with crusty bread.

smoked trout & horseradish pâté

Serves **4**
Preparation time **8 minutes**

8 oz **hot-smoked trout fillets**
1 teaspoon **paprika**
2 tablespoons **lemon juice**
2 tablespoons **hot**
  horseradish sauce
½ cup **cream cheese**
salt and **black pepper**
1 tablespoon **snipped chives**,
  to garnish
whole-wheat toast or
  crackers, to serve

Flake the fish, removing any small bones. Place in a food processor with all the remaining ingredients and blend to a coarse pâté, scraping down the sides of the bowl from time to time.

Season to taste, garnish with the chives, and serve with whole-wheat toast or crackers.

For smoked trout scrambled eggs, beat 6 eggs with 2 tablespoons milk and season to taste. Melt 1 tablespoon butter in a nonstick saucepan over low heat and add the eggs. Cook gently for 5–6 minutes, stirring occasionally, until the eggs are soft and creamy. Remove from the heat and stir in 8 oz flaked smoked trout and 1 tablespoon snipped chives. Serve immediately with whole-wheat toast.

poached eggs with spinach

Serves **4**
Preparation time **2 minutes**
Cooking time **8 minutes**

4 **vines of cherry tomatoes**,
  about 6 tomatoes on each
2 tablespoons **balsamic syrup**
  or **glaze**
1 **small bunch of basil**,
  leaves removed
1 tablespoon **vinegar**
4 extra-large **eggs**
3½ cups **baby spinach**
salt and **black pepper**
4 thick slices of **whole-wheat**
  toast, to serve

Preheat the oven to 400°F and bring a large saucepan of water to a gentle simmer. Place the cherry tomato vines in an ovenproof dish, drizzle with the balsamic syrup or glaze, sprinkle with the basil leaves, and season to taste. Cook in the preheated oven for 8 minutes, or until the tomatoes begin to collapse.

Meanwhile, add the vinegar to the pan of simmering water, carefully break 2 eggs into the water, and cook for 3 minutes. Remove with a slotted spoon and keep warm. Repeat with the remaining eggs.

Divide the spinach among 4 serving plates and place a poached egg on top of each. Arrange the tomatoes on the plates and drizzle the juices on top. Serve immediately with whole-wheat toast.

For boiled egg, spinach & sprout salad, boil 4 eggs in a saucepan of simmering water for 7–8 minutes. Meanwhile, divide 3½ cups baby spinach and 24 halved cherry tomatoes among 4 serving plates. Cool the eggs under cold running water and peel and slice thickly. Place the sliced eggs on top of the salads, sprinkle with ¾ cup alfalfa sprouts, and drizzle with a little olive oil and balsamic syrup. Serve with crusty bread.

moroccan-style hummus

Serves **4**
Preparation time **5 minutes**

1 (15 oz) can **chickpeas**,
   drained and rinsed
1 tablespoon **tahini paste**
1 **garlic clove**, peeled
¼ cup **Greek yogurt**
1 tablespoon **rose harissa
   paste**, plus extra to drizzle
2 tablespoons **lemon juice**
salt and **black pepper**
pita breads, to serve

Place all the ingredients in a food processor, reserving a few chickpeas for garnish, and blend to a smooth paste. If the consistency is too thick, you can add a little warm water.

Season to taste, transfer to a serving bowl, and garnish with the reserved chickpeas and a drizzle of extra harissa. Serve with warmed pita breads.

For Moroccan pan-roasted chickpeas, drain 1 (15 oz) can chickpeas and dry on paper towels. Place in a bowl and sprinkle with 2 tablespoons Moroccan spice mix, such as ras el hanout, and stir well to coat. Heat 2 tablespoons olive oil in a large skillet and cook the chickpeas for 5–6 minutes, stirring occasionally, until golden. Transfer to a bowl and serve hot or cold.

nachos with beans & cheese

Serves **4**
Preparation time **4 minutes**
Cooking time **3–4 minutes**

1 (7–8 oz) package **plain
    tortilla chips**
¾ cup **prepared fresh
    tomato salsa**
2 cups drained and rinsed,
    canned **mixed beans**, such
    as **red kidney beans, pinto
    beans, black beans,** and
    cannellini beans
1½ cups drained, canned
    sliced green jalapeños
1 cup shredded **mozzarella
    cheese**

To serve
sour cream
prepared guacamole

Place the tortilla chips in a shallow, ovenproof dish.
Spoon the salsa over the chips, followed by the mixed
beans, then sprinkle with the jalapeños and cheese.

Cook under a preheated hot broiler for 3–4 minutes,
until the cheese has melted. Serve immediately with
sour cream and guacamole.

For nachos with corn kernels & chicken, arrange
the tortilla chips in an ovenproof dish as above, spoon
the salsa over the chips, and sprinkle with 6 chopped
scallions. Drain 1 (8¾ oz) can corn kernels and sprinkle
over the top with 2 shredded, cooked chicken breasts.
Top with the shredded cheese and cook as above until
piping hot. Serve immediately.

chorizo, bean & tomato salad

Serves **4**
Preparation time **6 minutes**
Cooking time **3–4 minutes**

8 oz **chorizo**, sliced
1 (15 oz) **can lima beans**,
   drained and rinsed
16 **cherry tomatoes**
1 **small red onion**,
   thinly sliced
1 tablespoon **extra virgin
   olive oil**
1 tablespoon **sherry vinegar**
   or **red wine vinegar**
salt and **black pepper**
small handful of c**hopped
   flat-leaf parsley**, to garnish
crusty bread, to serve

Cook the chorizo in a large skillet over medium heat for 3–4 minutes, turning once, until crisp. Remove from the heat and stir in the lima beans, tomatoes, and red onion.

Whisk together the oil and vinegar in a small bowl and season to taste. Transfer the chorizo mixture to a serving dish, pour the dressing over the mixture, and toss well. Sprinkle with the parsley and serve immediately with crusty bread

For warm chorizo, chickpea & red pepper salad,
cook the chorizo as above, then stir in 1 (15 oz) drained, canned chickpeas. Remove from the heat and stir in 1 ½ cups drained and chopped roasted red peppers in oil and 2 tablespoons chopped fresh cilantro. Divide 1 (6 oz) package baby spinach among 4 bowls, top with the chickpea mixture, and serve each portion with a spoonful of Greek yogurt.

french toast

Serves **4**
Preparation time **5 minutes**
Cooking time **4 minutes**

2 **eggs**, beaten
1 teaspoon **vanilla extract**
½ cup **milk**
1 tablespoon **granulated sugar**, plus extra for sprinkling
½ teaspoon **ground cinnamon**
4 thick slices of **bread**
2 tablespoons **butter**

Whisk the eggs with the vanilla extract, milk, sugar, and cinnamon in a shallow dish. Place the slices of bread in the mixture, turning to coat both sides so that they absorb the liquid.

Heat the butter in a nonstick skillet. Use a spatula to transfer the soaked bread to the hot skillet and cook for 2 minutes on each side, until golden.

Cut the toasts in half diagonally, sprinkle with a little granulated sugar, and serve immediately with the sauce below. Alternatively, serve with a traditional drizzle of maple syrup.

For apple & raspberry sauce, to serve as an accompaniment, heat 2 tablespoons butter in a skillet, add 6 peeled, cored, and sliced Pippin apples, and cook for 2–3 minutes. Sprinkle 1 tablespoon light brown sugar, ½ teaspoon ground cinnamon, and 1 cup raspberries over the apples and cook gently for 1–2 minutes. Pour over the French toast and sprinkle with extra granulated sugar.

pasta, noodles & rice

spinach, ricotta & basil penne

Serves **4**
Preparation time **4 minutes**
Cooking time **6 minutes**

1 lb **fresh penne**
1 tablespoon **olive oil**
1 teaspoon **prepared chopped garlic**
1 (5 oz) package **spinach**, finely chopped
2 tablespoons **chopped basil**
1 cup **ricotta cheese**
½ cup **dry white wine**
salt and **black pepper**
Parmesan cheese shavings, to serve

Cook the pasta in a large saucepan of lightly salted boiling water for 3–4 minutes, or according to package directions, until al dente. Drain and return to the pan to keep warm.

Meanwhile, heat the oil in a large saucepan and cook the garlic for 2 minutes. Stir in the spinach and cook for 1–2 minutes, until wilted. Add the basil, ricotta, and wine, season to taste, and cook gently until the ricotta has melted.

Stir the drained pasta into the ricotta mixture, toss well, and divide among 4 bowls. Serve topped with Parmesan shavings and freshly ground black pepper.

For pea, ricotta & mint tagiatelle, cook 1 lb fresh tagliatelle in a large saucepan of lightly salted boiling water according to package directions, along with 2 cups frozen peas. Drain, reserving 2 tablespoons of the cooking water, and return to the pan. Stir in 1 cup ricotta cheese with the reserved water until you have a creamy sauce. Add the finely grated rind of 1 lemon, ¼ cup chopped mint, and ½ cup freshly grated Parmesan cheese and stir well. Serve immediately with freshly ground black pepper.

gnocchi with sage & pine nuts

Serves **4**
Preparation time **5 minutes**
Cooking time **2–3 minutes**

1 lb **fresh potato gnocchi**
4 tablespoons
   unsalted butter
12 **sage leaves**
¼ cup **pine nuts**
freshly ground black pepper

To serve
½ cup grated
   Parmesan cheese
crisp green salad

Cook the gnocchi in a large saucepan of lightly salted boiling water for 2–3 minutes, or according to package directions, until the gnocchi is plump and rises to the surface.

Meanwhile, heat the butter in a large skillet over moderate heat. When the butter starts to foam, stir in the sage leaves and pine nuts and cook for 1–2 minutes, until the sage is crispy and the pine nuts are golden. Add the gnocchi and toss to combine.

Divide among 4 bowls and serve sprinkled with the Parmesan and plenty of freshly ground black pepper. Serve with a crisp green salad.

For gnocchi with salami & spicy tomato sauce,
cut 8 oz salami slices into thin strips. Heat 1 tablespoon olive oil in a large skillet, add 1 teaspoon prepared minced garlic and the salami, and cook for 2–3 minutes. Stir in 1½ cups prepared tomato sauce with chile. Bring to a boil and simmer for 3–4 minutes. Meanwhile, cook 1 lb fresh gnocchi as above and drain well. Stir the gnocchi into the tomato sauce and serve immediately with freshly grated Parmesan cheese.

spicy thai crab noodles

Serves **2**
Preparation time **1 minute**
Cooking time **9 minutes**

1 tablespoon **peanut** or
  sunflower oil
2 tablespoons **Thai red
  curry paste**
1¾ cups **can coconut milk**
2 teaspoons **Thai fish sauce**
1 teaspoon **lemon grass
  paste**
2 **fresh** or **dried kaffir lime
  leaves**
1 cup **trimmed green beans**
8 oz **store-bought cooked
  egg noodles**
4 oz **cooked crabmeat**
2 tablespoons **prepared
  chopped cilantro** (optional)
6 **basil leaves**

Heat the oil in a medium saucepan, add the curry paste, and cook for 1 minute. Stir in the coconut milk and fish sauce.

Add the lemon grass paste, lime leaves, and green beans, cover, and simmer for about 6 minutes, until the beans are tender.

Stir in the noodles, crab, cilantro, if using, and basil. Cook for 2 minutes, until the noodles and crab are heated through. Divide between 2 bowls and serve immediately.

For spicy Thai shrimp, ginger & scallion stir-fry,
heat 1 tablespoon oil in a wok or large skillet and add 8 oz raw, peeled jumbo shrimp, 2 teaspoons prepared chopped ginger, 1 crushed garlic clove, 8 sliced scallions, and 1 seeded and chopped, small, fresh red chile. Stir-fry for 2–3 minutes, until the shrimp have turned pink. Add 3 tablespoons lime juice, 1 tablespoon Thai fish sauce, and 1 tablespoon light soy sauce. Stir-fry for 1 minute, then stir in 2 tablespoons chopped fresh cilantro. Serve immediately with prepared cooked noodles.

chinese fried rice

Serves **4**
Preparation time **3 minutes**
Cooking time **7 minutes**

2 **extra-large eggs**
2 teaspoons **sesame oil**
2 tablespoons **sunflower oil**
3 cups **cooked rice**
1 cup **frozen peas**
4 oz **cooked, peeled shrimp**
4 oz **smoked ham**, chopped
4 **scallions**, finely chopped
2 tablespoons **light soy sauce**

Beat the eggs in a small bowl with the sesame oil. Heat the sunflower oil in a wok or large skillet, add the rice, and stir-fry for 2 minutes, then add the peas, shrimp, and ham and cook for an additional 2–3 minutes.

Push the rice mixture to one side of the wok, then add the eggs. Let set for 10 seconds, then break up and stir into the rice. Add the scallions and soy sauce and stir-fry for an additional minute. Serve immediately.

For Chinese five spice rice with chicken & cashew nuts, heat 1 tablespoon sunflower oil in a wok or large skillet and add 12 oz chicken strips. Stir-fry for 2–3 minutes, until golden, then add ¾ cup unsalted cashew nuts and cook for 2 minutes. Add a bunch of chopped scallions and 1 cup bean sprouts and stir-fry for 2 minutes, then stir in 3 cups cooked rice. Add 1 teaspoon Chinese five spice powder and cook for 2 minutes, then add 2 tablespoons soy sauce. Stir to heat through and serve immediately.

sicilian spaghetti

Serves **4**
Preparation time **4 minutes**
Cooking time **6 minutes**

1 lb **fresh spaghetti**
2 (2 oz) **cans anchovy fillets
in olive oil**
2 teaspoons **prepared
chopped garlic**
⅓ cup **chopped flat-leaf
parsley**
¼ teaspoon **dried red pepper
flakes** (optional)
juice of 3 **lemons**
freshly ground black pepper
½ cup grated
Parmesan cheese
arugula salad, to serve

Cook the pasta in a large saucepan of unsalted boiling water for 3–4 minutes, or according to package directions, until al dente. Drain and return to the pan to keep warm.

Meanwhile, drain the olive oil from the cans of anchovies into a large skillet and add the garlic. Cook over moderate heat for 1 minute, then add the anchovies. Cook for 2–3 minutes, until the anchovies begin to soften and break up.

Add the parsley and red pepper flakes, if using, then stir in the lemon juice. Add the drained pasta to the skillet, season with black pepper, and toss to mix. Stir in most of the Parmesan, reserving a little for garnish. Divide the pasta among 4 bowls, sprinkle with the reserved Parmesan, and serve immediately with an arugula salad.

For penne with anchovy, tomato & olives, cook

1 lb fresh penne in a large saucepan of lightly salted boiling water according to package directions, drain, and return to the pan to keep warm. Drain the oil from 1 (2 oz) can of anchovies into a skillet with 2 teaspoons prepared chopped garlic. Cook for 1 minute, then add the anchovies and cook as above. Stir in 1½ cups prepared tomato sauce, simmer for 3–4 minutes to heat through, then stir in ½ cup sliced ripe black olives. Pour the sauce over the drained pasta, toss well, and serve immediately with freshly grated Parmesan cheese and torn basil leaves.

spicy shrimp jambalaya

Serves **4**
Preparation time **2 minutes**
Cooking time **8 minutes**

1 tablespoon **olive oil**
3 oz **prepared diced chorizo**
1 **prepared chopped onion**
1 teaspoon **prepared chopped garlic**
½ **red bell pepper**, cored, seeded, and chopped
½ **green bell pepper**, cored, seeded, and chopped
1 teaspoon **hot chili powder**
1 teaspoon **turmeric**
1 teaspoon **dried mixed herbs**
3 cups **cooked rice**
1 (14½ oz) can **diced tomatoes**
⅔ cup **chicken stock**, made with boiling water
12 oz **cooked, peeled jumbo shrimp**
Tabasco sauce, to taste
salt and **black pepper**
scallions, chopped, to garnish

Heat the oil in a large saucepan, add the chorizo, onion, garlic, and bell peppers, and cook for 2 minutes, until the onion has softened and the chorizo has released its oil.

Add the spices and herbs, then stir in the rice and cook for 1 minute. Stir in the diced tomatoes and chicken stock, bring to a boil, and simmer for 4–5 minutes.

Stir in the shrimp and heat through, then season to taste with salt, black pepper, and a few drops of Tabasco sauce. Divide among 4 bowls and serve immediately, garnished with chopped scallions.

For chorizo & tomato rice, heat 1 tablespoon olive oil in a saucepan and add 6 oz prepared diced chorizo, 1 prepared chopped onion, 1 sliced red bell pepper, and 1 teaspoon prepared chopped garlic. Cook for 3–4 minutes, until the oil has been released from the chorizo. Stir in 3 cups cooked rice and pour ⅔ cup dry white wine over the top. Bring to a boil and simmer for 2 minutes. Stir in 1 (14½ oz) can diced tomatoes with herbs and cook for an additional 2–3 minutes. Season to taste, stir in 2 tablespoons chopped parsley, and serve immediately.

vietnamese chicken noodle salad

Serves **4**
Preparation time **7 minutes**
Cooking time **3 minutes**

5 oz **rice vermicelli**
½ **cucumber**, cut in half
   lengthwise
8 oz **cooked chicken breast**,
   shredded (about 2 cups)
2 **carrots**, cut into thin strips
¾ cup **bean sprouts**
¼ cup **chopped mint**, plus
   extra to garnish
¼ cup **chopped fresh
   cilantro**, plus extra to garnish
½ cup chopped
   roasted peanuts

Dressing
2 tablespoons **rice wine
   vinegar**
3 tablespoons **sweet chili
   sauce**
1 tablespoon **Thai fish sauce**
¼ cup **lime juice**

Prepare the vermicelli according to the package directions, then refresh under cold water and let drain.

Meanwhile, remove the seeds from the cucumber, using a teaspoon, and thinly slice to form crescents. Place in a bowl with the chicken, carrots, bean sprouts, chopped herbs, and peanuts, then added the drained noodles and toss well.

Whisk together all the dressing ingredients, then pour the dressing over the noodles and stir well. Serve garnished with extra cilantro and mint leaves.

For crab & mango rice noodle salad, prepare the noodles as above, then toss in a bowl with 1 peeled, pitted, and chopped mango, 2 (6 oz) cans white crabmeat, drained, 2 cups arugula, and ¼ cup chopped fresh cilantro. Whisk together 3 tablespoons lime juice, 1 tablespoon sunflower oil, ½ seeded and chopped red chile, and ½ teaspoon granulated sugar. Season to taste and pour the dressing over the noodles.

asian pesto with soba noodles

Serves **4**
Preparation time **4 minutes**
Cooking time **5–6 minutes**

12 oz **soba noodles**
2 **lemon grass stalks**
2 **small fresh red chiles**,
  seeded and chopped
finely grated rind and juice of
  1 **lime**
2 cups **fresh cilantro leaves**
1 cup **basil leaves**
2 teaspoons **prepared
  chopped ginger**
1 **garlic clove**, peeled
½ cup **roasted peanuts**
⅓ cup **peanut oil**
2 teaspoons **Thai fish sauce**
lime wedges, to serve

Cook the noodles in a large saucepan of lightly salted boiling water according to package directions, until al dente. Drain and return to the pan to keep warm.

Meanwhile, remove the tough outer leaves from the lemon grass and coarsely chop the core. Place in a food processor with all the remaining ingredients, except the oil and fish sauce, and blend to a smooth paste, scraping down the sides of the bowl with a spatula from time to time. With the processor still running, add the oil and fish sauce.

Stir the pesto into the warm noodles, divide among 4 bowls, and serve immediately with lime wedges.

For arugula pesto, place 1 (5 oz) package arugula in a food processor with ½ cup chopped toasted hazelnuts, 2 peeled garlic cloves, and ½ cup grated Parmesan cheese. Blend to a paste, then gradually add ⅓ cup olive oil. Season to taste and serve with fresh pasta or gnocchi.

thai chicken & basil fried rice

Serves **4**
Preparation time **3 minutes**
Cooking time **7 minutes**

2 tablespoons **peanut oil**
3 **garlic cloves**, chopped
3 **shallots**, thinly sliced
3 **small fresh red chiles**,
  finely chopped
2 **red bell peppers**, cored,
  seeded, and diced
8 oz **ground chicken**
3 tablespoons **Thai fish sauce**
½ teaspoon **brown sugar**
2 tablespoons **light soy sauce**
3 cups **cooked rice**
large handful of **basil**

Heat the oil in a wok over high heat until the oil starts to shimmer. Add the garlic, shallots, chiles, and red bell peppers and stir-fry for 30 seconds, then add the chicken, fish sauce, sugar, and soy sauce.

Stir-fry for 3–4 minutes, breaking the chicken up with the spatula, until the chicken is browned and cooked through.

Add the rice and basil and stir gently until piping hot. Serve immediately.

For pork & herb fried rice, chop 8 oz lean pork into small cubes and use in place of the chicken. Cook as above, reducing the basil by half and adding a handful of cilantro leaves and 6 torn mint leaves.

spicy chicken satay noodles

Serves **2**

Preparation time **4 minutes**

Cooking time **6 minutes**

1 tablespoon **sunflower oil**

1 teaspoon **prepared chopped ginger**

5 oz **cooked chicken**, diced (about 1 cup)

4 **scallions**, thinly sliced

¾ cup **bean sprouts**

10 oz **store-bought cooked medium egg noodles**

fresh cilantro, to garnish

Sauce

¼ cup **chunky peanut butter**

2 tablespoons **sweet chili sauce**

2 tablespoons **dark soy sauce**

2 tablespoons **lime juice**

½ cup **water**

Whisk together all the ingredients for the sauce except the water in a small bowl.

Heat the oil in a wok or large skillet, add the ginger, and cook for 1 minute. Stir in the chicken, scallions, and bean sprouts and stir-fry for 2 minutes. Add the noodles and stir-fry for 1 minute.

Pour in the sauce and measured water and stir to coat the noodles and chicken. Heat until piping hot, then serve immediately garnished with cilantro leaves.

For spicy shrimp noodle salad, mix 2 tablespoons peanut butter with 1 teaspoon sesame oil, 1 tablespoon chili sauce, and 2 tablespoons boiling water to make a dressing. Put 8 oz cooked, peeled shrimp in a bowl with 10 oz store-bought cooked noodles, 2 sliced scallions, 1 cup halved snow peas, and ½ seeded and sliced red bell pepper. Pour the dressing over the salad and toss to mix. Serve garnished with a handful of chopped roasted peanuts.

orzo risotto with pancetta & peas

Serves **4**
Preparation time **1 minute**
Cooking time **9 minutes**

3¾ cups **chicken** or
vegetable stock, made with
boiling water if from
a bouillon cube
12 oz **orzo** or other small
soup pasta shapes
(about 2 cups)
1 tablespoon **butter**
1 teaspoon **prepared**
chopped garlic
5 oz **diced pancetta**
1⅓ cups **frozen peas**
handful of **parsley,** chopped
1 cup grated **Parmesan**
cheese
salt and **black pepper**

Place the stock in a medium nonstick saucepan, bring back to a boil, and add the pasta.

Meanwhile, melt the butter in a small skillet and add the garlic and pancetta. Sauté for 2 minutes, until the pancetta is crispy.

Add the pancetta and garlic to the orzo with the peas and continue to cook over moderate heat for about 7 minutes, until al dente, stirring from time to time to prevent the pasta from sticking and adding a little more water, if necessary.

Season to taste and stir in the parsley and most of the Parmesan, reserving a little for garnish. Serve immediately, sprinkled with the reserved Parmesan and freshly ground black pepper.

For orzo risotto with goat cheese, pancetta & sage,
cook the pasta in a boiling stock as above. Meanwhile, cook 1 sliced red onion in the butter with the garlic and pancetta until softened, then stir into the orzo. When the pasta is al dente, stir in 4 oz soft goat cheese, 2 tablespoons chopped sage, and ½ cup freshly grated Parmesan cheese. Season and serve immediately with freshly ground black pepper.

chicken & noodle miso soup

Serves **4**
Preparation time **2 minutes**
Cooking time **8 minutes**

3¾ cups **chicken stock**, made
with boiling water if using a
bouillon cube
2 (¾ oz) **envelopes**
miso soup paste or
2 tablespoons **miso paste**
2 teaspoons p**repared**
chopped ginger
4 **scallions**, cut into thin strips
1 **carrot**, cut into thin strips
4 **baby bok choy**, halved
8 oz **cooked chicken breast**,
sliced (about 1½ cups)
10 oz **store-bought cooked**
medium egg noodles

Place the chicken stock, miso paste, and ginger in a
medium saucepan and bring back to a boil. Simmer for
2 minutes.

Add the scallions, carrot, bok choy, and chicken and
simmer for 3–4 minutes more.

Stir in the noodles and cook for an additional
2 minutes to heat through. Divide among 4 bowls
and serve immediately.

For tofu & noodle miso soup, dissolve 1½ teaspoons
dashi (bonito flavored granules) in 5 cups boiling
water or chicken stock in a medium saucepan and
add 2 (¾ oz) envelopes miso paste and 1 tablespoon
wakame (dried seaweed). Bring to a boil and add
8 oz store-bought cooked egg noodles and 8 oz
diced tofu. Simmer for 2–3 minutes, then stir in
2 tablespoons chopped scallions. Divide among
4 bowls and serve immediately.

ham & shrimp fried rice

Serves **2–3**
Preparation time **3 minutes**
Cooking time **7 minutes**

4 **eggs**
1½ teaspoons **sesame oil**
2 teaspoons **light soy sauce**
1 tablespoon **peanut oil**
4 oz **raw, peeled shrimp**
4 oz **ham**, shredded
1 tablespoon **prepared
   chopped ginger**
2 **garlic cloves**, crushed
5 **scallions**, finely sliced
2 cups **cooked rice**
salt

Break the eggs into a bowl with 1 teaspoon of the sesame oil, the soy sauce, and a pinch of salt and whisk lightly to combine.

Heat half the peanut oil in a wok or large skillet over high heat until the oil starts to shimmer. Pour in the egg mixture and use a spatula to scramble it for 30–60 seconds, until just cooked, then remove from the wok and set aside.

Return the wok to the heat and heat the remaining oil. Add the shrimp, ham, ginger, and garlic and stir-fry for 1 minute, until the shrimp turn pink. Add the scallions, rice, eggs, and the remaining sesame oil and stir-fry for about 3 minutes, until piping hot. Season to taste and serve immediately.

For chicken fried rice, omit the shrimp and ham. Cook the eggs as above and remove from the wok, then heat 1 tablespoon peanut oil and stir-fry the ginger, garlic, and 8 oz finely chopped chicken breast (about 1½ cups) for 2–3 minutes. Add 2 tablespoons oyster sauce and cook for 1 minute, then add the scallions and rice and continue as above.

smoked haddock kedgeree

Serves **4**
Preparation time **3 minutes**
Cooking time **6–7 minutes**

1 lb **smoked haddock fillet**
1 tablespoon **sunflower oil**
1 tablespooon **butter**
4 teaspoons **mild curry powder**
3 cups **cooked rice**
2 tablespoons **lemon juice**
2 tablespoons **prepared chopped parsley**
4 **eggs**

Place the fish in a saucepan and pour boiling water over it to just cover. Cook over moderate heat for 3 minutes.

Meanwhile, heat the oil and butter in a large, nonstick skillet with a lid and add the curry powder. Cook for 1 minute, then add the rice and stir-fry for 2 minutes.

Remove the fish from the skillet and flake into large pieces, removing any skin and bones. Stir into the rice along with 3 tablespoons of the cooking liquid, the lemon juice, and parsley.

Make 4 wells in the rice and break in the eggs, cover the pan with the lid, and cook over low heat for 2–3 minutes, until the egg whites are just set. Serve immediately.

For curried vegetable rice, heat 1 tablespoon oil in a wok or large skillet, add 1 prepared chopped onion, and cook for 2–3 minutes, until softened. Stir in 2 tablespoons curry paste, then add 12 oz frozen mixed vegetables. Cook for 2 minutes, then stir in 3 cups cooked rice. Add ⅔ cup boiling vegetable stock, then cover and simmer for 4 minutes, until the vegetables are tender. Stir in 3 tablespoons plain yogurt and ¼ cup chopped fresh cilantro and season to taste. Serve immediately with mango chutney.

pasta with tomatoes & basil

Serves **4**
Preparation time **2 minutes**
Cooking time **8 minutes**

2 tablespoons **olive oil**
1 **onion**, finely chopped
1 teaspoon **prepared chopped garlic**
3 cups **cherry tomatoes**
1 teaspoon **sugar**
1 teaspoon **balsamic vinegar**
10 **basil leaves**, shredded
12 oz **angel hair spaghetti**
salt and **black pepper**

To serve
freshly grated
   Parmesan cheese
arugula

Heat the oil in a large skillet, add the onion and garlic, and cook for 2–3 minutes, until the onion has softened. Stir in the cherry tomatoes, sugar, and vinegar and cook for 5 minutes, stirring occasionally, until the tomatoes have softened and start to collapse. Gently squash some of them with the back of a spoon and season to taste. Stir in the basil.

Meanwhile, cook the pasta in a saucepan of lightly salted boiling water according to package directions until al dente.

Drain the pasta and toss with the sauce. Serve immediately with the grated Parmesan and arugula.

For pasta with creamy tomatoes & zucchini,
heat 1 tablespoon olive oil in a skillet and cook 2 chopped zucchini and 1 teaspoon prepared chopped garlic for 2–3 minutes. Add 1 cup mascarpone cheese and stir in until melted, then add 1 cup tomato puree or tomato sauce with herbs. Season and simmer for 2–3 minutes. Meanwhile, cook 1 lb fresh penne according to package directions until al dente. Drain well, then stir into the sauce. Serve immediately with freshly ground black pepper.

egg fried rice

Serves **2**
Preparation time **3 minutes**
Cooking time **3–4 minutes**

2 tablespoons **peanut oil**
4 **eggs**
2 teaspoons **prepared chopped ginger**
1½ tablespoons **light soy sauce**
2 cups **cooked rice**
2 **scallions**, finely sliced
¼ teaspoon **sesame oil**

Heat the peanut oil in a wok or large skillet over high heat until the oil starts to shimmer. Meanwhile, beat the eggs with the ginger and half the soy sauce.

Pour the egg mixture into the wok and use a spatula to scramble it for 30–60 seconds, until just cooked. Add the rice, scallions, sesame oil, and remaining soy sauce and stir-fry for 1–2 minutes, until piping hot. Serve immediately.

For fried rice with Chinese cabbage & chile,
follow the recipe above, adding 1 sliced fresh red chile and 2 cups shredded Chinese cabbage once the rice is hot, and stir-fry for an additional 30 seconds. Serve immediately.

meaty treats

parmesan & basil chicken

Serves 2
Preparation time **4 minutes**
Cooking time **6 minutes**

2 thin **chicken cutlets**, about
¼ inch thick
¼ cup **all-purpose flour**
½ cup **fresh white bread
crumbs**
¼ cup grated **Parmesan
cheese**
2 tablespoons chopped **basil**
1 **egg**, beaten
1 tablespoon **olive oil**
salt and **black pepper**

To serve
crisp green salad
lemon wedges

Season the chicken, then dust both sides in the flour, shaking off any excess.

Mix the bread crumbs, Parmesan, and basil in a shallow dish. Place the beaten egg in another shallow dish.

Dip the chicken in the beaten egg on both sides, then in the Parmesan bread crumbs to form an even coating.

Meanwhile, heat the oil in a large skillet. When hot, add the coated chicken and cook for 3 minutes on each side, until crispy, browned, and cooked through. Serve immediately with a crisp green salad and lemon wedges.

For chicken cutlets with caper sauce, heat 1 tablespoon oil in a large skillet. Season 2 thin chicken cutlets with freshly ground black pepper and cook for 3 minutes on each side, until cooked through. Remove from the skillet and keep warm. Add ½ cup boiling chicken stock to the skillet with ¼ cup white wine and simmer rapidly for 1 minute. Remove from the heat and whisk in 1 tablespoon capers and 1 tablespoon butter. Season, pour the sauce over the cutlets, and serve with cooked rice.

pepper steak with marsala sauce

Serves **2**
Preparation time **1 minute**
Cooking time **6–9 minutes**

1 teaspoon **sunflower oil**
1 tablespoon **butter**
1 tablespoon **mixed peppercorns**, crushed
2 **sirloin** or **tenderloin steaks**, about ½ inch thick
2 cups **prepared sliced mushrooms**
2 tablespoons **marsala** or other **red wine**
⅓ cup **sour cream**
salt
snow peas, to serve

Heat the oil and butter in a large skillet. Press the peppercorns on both sides of the steaks to form an even coating.

Place the mushrooms and steaks in the hot skillet and cook the steaks for 2 minutes each side for rare or 3–4 minutes each side for medium to well done, stirring the mushrooms occasionally. Remove the steaks from the skillet and keep warm.

Add the marsala to the skillet and cook for 1 minute, then stir in the sour cream and cook over low heat until the sauce thickens. Season with salt, pour the sauce over the steaks, and serve with snow peas.

For steaks with blue cheese sauce, mix 2 oz soft blue cheese with 1 tablespoon crème fraîche or sour cream and 1 tablespoon chopped chives. Season the steaks on both sides with freshly ground black pepper and place on a baking sheet. Cook under a preheated hot broiler for 3–4 minutes on one side, depending how you like your steak cooked, then turn over. Broil for an additional 2–3 minutes, then spread the cheese mixture over the tops of the steaks. Broil for an additional minute until the cheese has melted. Transfer to serving plates and pour over any cheesy juices from the baking sheet. Serve with mashed potatoes

pork with apple & cider sauce

Serves **2**
Preparation time **3 minutes**
Cooking time **7 minutes**

1 tablespoon **oil**
1 tablespoon **unsalted butter**
8 oz **pork tenderloin**, cut into
  ½-inch thick slices
1 **Pippin apple**, cored and cut
  into wedges
⅔ cup **cider** or **apple juice**
¼ cup **crème fraîche**
  or **sour cream**
6 **sage leaves**, chopped
salt and **black pepper**
cooked rice, to serve

Heat the oil and butter in a large skillet over high heat. Add the pork tenderloins and brown for 1–2 minutes on each side.

Add the apple wedges with the cider or apple juice, bring to a boil, and simmer, uncovered, for 5 minutes, until the liquid has reduced and the pork is cooked through.

Stir in the crème fraîche and sage, season to taste, then simmer for 1 minute, until heated through. Serve with rice.

For Cantonese pork, thinly slice 8 oz pork tenderloin. Mix 1 teaspoon prepared chopped garlic with 3 tablespoons hoisin sauce, 2 tablespoons dark soy sauce, 1 tablespoon sherry, 1 tablespoon honey, and ½ teaspoon sesame oil. Heat 1 tablespoon oil in a wok over high heat, add the pork, and cook until browned. Stir in the sauce, simmer for 3 minutes, then stir in 1 bunch sliced scallions and 1 cup thin, short cucumber sticks. Heat through and serve immediately with cooked rice.

smoked chicken salad

Serves **4**
Preparation time **8 minutes**
Cooking time **1–2 minutes**

¼ cup **pumpkin seeds**
12 oz **skinless smoked chicken breast**, shredded (about 2 cups)
2 **red onions**, finely sliced and rinsed in water
12 **cherry tomatoes**, halved
3 cups **mixed salad greens**
crusty bread, to serve

Dressing
1 **avocado**, peeled, pitted, and diced
2 tablespoons **lime juice**
1 tablespoon **Dijon mustard**
salt and **black pepper**

Heat a small skillet until hot, add the pumpkin seeds, and dry-fry for 1–2 minutes, stirring occasionally, until browned.

Make the dressing by placing all the ingredients in a food processor and blending them until smooth. Season to taste.

Place the chicken, onions, tomatoes, pumpkin seeds, and salad greens in a salad bowl and toss together. Drizzle with the dressing and serve with crusty bread.

For smoked chicken, broccoli & pasta salad,

cook 8 oz fresh rigatoni in lightly salted boiling water according to package directions, adding 3½ cups small broccoli florets for the final 3 minutes of cooking. Drain and refresh under cold running water, then drain again. Prepare the salad as above, adding the pasta and broccoli instead of the pumpkin seeds and red onions. Make the dressing as above. Arrange the salad greens in 4 serving bowls, top with the pasta salad, and drizzle with the dressing.

stir-fried lamb with ginger & garlic

Serves **4**
Preparation time **3 minutes**
Cooking time **6 minutes**

1 lb **lamb** or **beef strips**
1 tablespoon **Chinese rice wine** or **dry sherry**
2 tablespoons **dark soy sauce**
1 teaspoon **sesame oil**
2 teaspoons **prepared chopped garlic**
2 teaspoons **prepared chopped ginger**
2 teaspoons **cornstarch**
1 tablespoon **sunflower oil**
6 **scallions**, sliced lengthwise
cooked noodles, to serve

Place the lamb or beef in a bowl and stir in the rice wine, soy sauce, sesame oil, garlic, ginger, and cornstarch. Mix well.

Heat the oil in a wok or large skillet over high heat. When it is hot, add the lamb and sauce and stir-fry for 2–3 minutes, until browned.

Add the scallions and stir-fry for an additional 2–3 minutes, until the sauce coats the meat. Serve immediately with noodles.

For grilled lamb with herbs & garlic, mix 1 teaspoon prepared chopped garlic with 2 tablespoons olive oil, 2 tablespoons lemon juice, and 1 teaspoon each of dried oregano and thyme. Add 4 lamb cutlets and coat in the mixture. Heat a ridged grill pan over high heat, add the lamb, and cook for 3–4 minutes each side. Serve with a mixed salad.

thai chicken with lemon grass

Serves **4**
Preparation time **2 minutes**
Cooking time **7–8 minutes**

2 **lemon grass stalks**
1¾ cups **coconut milk**
1 teaspoon **prepared chopped garlic**
2 teaspoons **prepared chopped ginger**
2 teaspoons **prepared chopped red chile**
2 teaspoons **brown sugar**
6 **kaffir lime leaves**
2 teaspoons **Thai fish sauce**
1 lb **chicken strips**
2 tablespoons **lime juice**
handful of **fresh cilantro** or **basil leaves**

Remove the tough outer leaves from the lemon grass and chop the core into 1 inch pieces. Place in a large saucepan with the coconut milk, garlic, ginger, chile, sugar, lime leaves, and fish sauce.

Bring to a boil and reduce the heat to a simmer. Add the chicken, partly cover with a lid, and cook gently for 6–7 minutes.

Stir in the lime juice and herbs and serve immediately.

For Thai chicken curry, cut 12 oz new potatoes into small pieces and cook in a saucepan of lightly salted boiling water for 4 minutes, until tender. Meanwhile, heat 1 tablespoon oil in a saucepan and add 1 lb chicken strips and 3 tablespoons Thai curry paste. Cook for 3–4 minutes, until the chicken is browned. Add 1¾ cups coconut milk, 2 kaffir lime leaves, and 1 teaspoon Thai fish sauce. Bring to a boil, stir in the potatoes, cover, and simmer for 5 minutes. Serve garnished with a large handful of unsalted peanuts.

sweet & sour ground pork

Serves **4**
Preparation time **1 minute**
Cooking time **8–9 minutes**

1 tablespoon **sunflower oil**
1 lb **lean ground pork**
1 **prepared chopped onion**
1 (8 oz) **can pineapple
    chunks in natural juice**
1 **red bell pepper**, cored,
    seeded, and chopped
cooked noodles, to serve

Sauce
¼ cup **ketchup**
1 tablespoon **prepared
    chopped ginger**
2 teaspoons **cornstarch**
2 tablespoons **dark soy sauce**
2 tablespoons **rice
    wine vinegar**
1 tablespoon **brown sugar**

Heat the oil in a wok or large skillet over high heat. Add the pork and onion and stir-fry for about 4 minutes, until the pork is cooked through.

Meanwhile, drain the pineapple, reserving the juice from the can. Whisk the pineapple juice with all the sauce ingredients and set aside.

Add the bell pepper and pineapple to the wok and stir-fry for 2–3 minutes, then pour in the sauce. Cook, stirring continuously, until the sauce thickens. Serve immediately with noodles.

For spicy Bombay ground pork, cut 8 oz new potatoes into ½ inch dice and cook in lightly salted boiling water for 4 minutes. Meanwhile, heat 1 tablespoon oil in a large wok or skillet over high heat and add 1 prepared chopped onion and 1 lb ground pork. Cook for 3–4 minutes, then add 3 tablespoons medium curry paste. Stir in the potatoes, 1 cup canned diced tomatoes, 1⅓ cups frozen peas, and ⅔ cup boiling chicken stock. Bring to a boil, reduce the heat, cover, and simmer for 4 minutes, stirring occasionally. Season to taste and serve with naan or pita bread.

thai red beef curry

Serves **4**
Preparation time **2 minutes**
Cooking time **8 minutes**

1 tablespoon **peanut oil**
1¼ lb **beef strips**
2 tablespoons **Thai red curry paste**
1¾ cups **coconut milk**
⅔ cup **beef stock**
1 tablespoon **brown sugar**
1 tablespoon **prepared chopped ginger**
1 **lemon grass stalk**, bruised
2 cups diagonally sliced **snow peas**
1 cup **bean sprouts**
1 tablespoon **Thai fish sauce**
1 tablespoon **lime juice**
small handful of **fresh cilantro**

Heat the oil in a wok or large skillet over high heat. Add the beef and curry paste and stir-fry for about 2 minutes, until the beef is lightly browned.

Add the coconut milk, stock, sugar, ginger, lemon grass, snow peas, bean sprouts, fish sauce, and lime juice. Bring to a boil, then reduce the heat and simmer for 2 minutes, until the snow peas are tender.

Remove the lemon grass from the curry and stir in the cilantro.

For Thai red vegetable curry, omit the beef and replace with 1 diced eggplant, 12 baby corn, and ¼ cup drained, canned bamboo shoots. Sauté the curry paste in the oil for 1 minute, then add the vegetables and other ingredients as above. Simmer for about 7 minutes, until the eggplant is tender.

duck & edamame salad

Serves **4**
Preparation time **6 minutes**
Cooking time **3–4 minutes**

1⅓ cups **fresh** or **frozen
edamame (soybeans)**
1 lb **store-bought cooked
Peking duck**, shredded
(about 3½ cups)
1 **cucumber**, finely sliced
5 **scallions**, very finely sliced,
plus extra to garnish
Sichuan pepper, to garnish

Dressing
2 tablespoons **hoisin sauce**
¼ cup **dark soy sauce**
3 tablespoons **lime juice**

Cook the edamame in a saucepan of lightly salted boiling water for 3–4 minutes, or according to package directions. Drain, refresh under cold running water, and drain again.

Toss the duck with the edamame, cucumber, and scallions in a large salad bowl. Make the dressing by whisking together all the ingredients.

Drizzle the dressing over the duck salad and toss gently to combine. Garnish with scallions and a sprinkling of Sichuan pepper and serve immediately.

For poached salmon & green bean salad, cook 3 cups green beans in a saucepan of lightly salted boiling water for 3–4 minutes. Drain, refresh under cold running water, and drain again. Meanwhile, cook 3 boneless, skinless salmon fillets, about 6 oz each, in a saucepan of lightly salted boiling water for 3–4 minutes, until just cooked but still pink in the middle. Flake the salmon into a salad bowl with the green beans, ½ finely diced cucumber, and 3 cups arugula and toss gently. Whisk together 2 tablespoons sweet chili sauce, 2 tablespoons soy sauce, and 3 tablespoons lime juice, drizzle the dressing over the salad, and serve immediately.

ham steaks with pineapple

Serves **2**
Preparation time **1 minute**
Cooking time **9 minutes**

2 **cured ham steaks**, about
  8 oz each
2 **canned pineapple slices**
mixed salad, to serve

Topping
⅓ cup **fresh white**
  bread crumbs
½ cup shredded **sharp**
  cheddar cheese
1 tablespoon **butter**, melted
2 tablespoons chopped
  flat-leaf parsley

Place the ham steaks on a baking sheet, snip the rinds at intervals to prevent them from curling, if needed, and cook under a preheated hot broiler for 5 minutes on one side. Meanwhile, mix together all the topping ingredients in a small bowl.

Turn over the steaks and place a pineapple slice on top of each. Return to the broiler and cook for 2 minutes, then top with the cheese mixture and cook for an additional 2 minutes, until the topping is golden. Serve with a mixed salad.

For maple & mustard ham steaks with fried eggs,
mix 2 tablespoons maple syrup with 2 tablespoons whole-grain mustard. Spread half the mixture over one side of 2 cured ham steaks and cook under a preheated hot broiler for 5 minutes. Turn the steaks over and spread with the remaining glaze. Cook for an additional 4 minutes, until glazed and sticky. Meanwhile, heat 1 tablespoon sunflower oil in a large skillet until hot, break 2 extra-large eggs into the skillet, and cook for 2–3 minutes. Serve the eggs with the ham and some crusty bread.

creamy paprika chicken

Serves **4**
Preparation time **1 minute**
Cooking time **9 minutes**

1 tablespoon **unsalted butter**
1 tablespoon **sunflower oil**
1 lb **chicken strips**
1 **red bell pepper**, cored,
  seeded, and sliced
2 tablespoons **sweet paprika**
½ cup **medium dry sherry**
2 teaspoons **tomato paste**
¼ cup **crème fraîche** or
  sour cream
1 tablespoon **prepared
  chopped parsley**
salt and **black pepper**
cooked rice, to serve

Heat the butter and oil in a large skillet and stir-fry the chicken strips for 3 minutes over high heat, until lightly browned.

Add the sliced red bell pepper and paprika and cook for 2 minutes, then add the sherry and tomato paste, bring to a boil, and simmer for 2–3 minutes.

Stir in the crème fraîche or sour cream and parsley, season to taste, and heat through. Serve with rice.

For creamy pesto chicken with lemon, cook 1 lb fresh penne in a saucepan of lightly salted boiling water according to package directions. Meanwhile, heat 1 tablespoon olive oil in a skillet with a lid, add 1 lb chicken strips, and cook for 3 minutes, until lightly browned. Stir in the finely grated rind of 1 lemon, the juice of 2 lemons, and 2 tablespoons fresh pesto sauce. Simmer for 1 minute, then stir in 3 tablespoons crème fraîche or heavy cream. Cover and simmer for 3–4 minutes. Drain the pasta, stir into the chicken mixture, and season to taste. Serve immediately.

veal with sage & prosciutto

Serves **2**
Preparation time **3 minutes**
Cooking time **7 minutes**

6 **sage leaves**
2 **veal cutlets**, about 4 oz
   each, pounded thinly with
   a meat mallet or rolling pin
4 slices of **prosciutto**
1 tablespoon **olive oil**
½ cup **chicken stock**
juice of 2 **lemons**
salt and **black pepper**
green beans, to serve

Place 3 sage leaves on top of each cutlet, season with black pepper, then wrap each cutlet in 2 slices of ham.

Heat the oil in a large skillet and cook the veal over high heat for 2 minutes on each side, until the veal is crispy. Transfer them to a warmed serving plate.

Pour the stock into the skillet and bring to a boil, stirring to incorporate all the juices from the veal. Reduce the stock by half, add the lemon juice, and simmer for 1 minute. Season to taste, pour the sauce over the veal, and serve with green beans.

For veal & mushroom stroganoff, cut the veal cutlets into thin strips. Heat 1 tablespoon oil in a skillet and stir-fry the veal with 1 teaspoon prepared chopped garlic for 2 minutes. Add 2 cups sliced mushrooms and cook for an additional 3 minutes. Stir in ⅔ cup sour cream and 1 teaspoon Dijon mustard. Simmer for 3–4 minutes, then stir in 2 tablespoons chopped parsley. Season to taste and serve immediately with rice.

sausages with popovers

Serves **4**
Preparation time **2 minutes**
Cooking time **8 minutes**

1 tablespoon **sunflower oil**
24 **miniature sausages**
 or 8 **link sausages**, cut
 into thirds
8 oz **new potatoes**, cut into
 ¾ inch dice
8 prepared **popovers**
2 tablespoons **crispy
 dried onions**
4 teaspoons **gravy granules**
1¼ cups **boiling water**
salt
frozen peas, to serve

Preheat the oven to 400°F. Heat the oil in a large skillet and cook the sausages for 7–8 minutes, turning occasionally, until cooked through.

Meanwhile, cook the potatoes in a saucepan of lightly salted boiling water for 5–6 minutes, until tender. Reheat the popovers in the preheated oven for 3–4 minutes.

Place the dried onions and gravy granules in a heatproof bowl, add a boiling water, and stir until dissolved. Add the potatoes and onion gravy to the sausages and stir to heat through.

Arrange the popovers on 4 serving plates and divide the sausage mixture among them. Serve immediately with peas.

For frankfurters with Boston beans, heat 1 tablespoon oil in a large saucepan, add 1 prepared chopped onion, and cook for 2–3 minutes, until softened. Meanwhile, cut 8 frankfurters into 1 inch chunks. Add to the pan and cook for 2 minutes. Stir in 1 (15 oz) can baked beans, 1 cup canned diced tomatoes, 1 teaspoon English mustard, and 1 tablespoon Worcestershire sauce. Bring to a boil, cover, and simmer for 4–5 minutes. Serve with crusty bread.

spicy cajun popcorn chicken

Serves **2**
Preparation time **4 minutes**
Cooking time **6 minutes**

⅔ cup **sunflower oil**
1 **egg white**
⅓ cup **buttermilk**
1 teaspoon **smoked paprika**
8 oz **diced chicken breast**
⅓ cup **all-purpose flour**
2 tablespoons **Cajun seasoning**
salt and **black pepper**

Chive mayonnaise
⅓ cup **mayonnaise**
2 tablespoons **snipped chives**

Heat the oil in a deep fryer or deep, heavy saucepan to 350°F, or until a cube of bread browns in 15 seconds.

Meanwhile, lightly beat the egg white in a shallow dish and stir in the buttermilk and paprika. Season to taste then add the chicken and stir to coat. Mix the flour with the Cajun seasoning in another bowl.

Dip the pieces of chicken in the seasoned flour, then deep-fry for 3–4 minutes, until golden brown. Remove with a slotted spoon and drain on paper towels.

Mix the mayonnaise with the chives and serve with the crispy chicken.

For spicy chicken fajitas, heat 1 tablespoon oil in a large skillet and stir-fry 8 oz chicken strips for 3–4 minutes, until browned. Add 1 sliced red bell pepper and ½ sliced onion and cook for 2–3 minutes. Stir in 2 tablespoons Mexican spice mix and cook for 2 minutes, then add 2 tablespoons lime juice. Divide the mixture among 4 warmed soft flour tortillas and add a spoonful of sour cream and prepared tomato salsa to each. Roll up and serve immediately.

pan-fried gnocchi & chorizo salad

Serves **4**
Preparation time **2 minutes**
Cooking time **8 minutes**

2 tablespoons **olive oil**
1 lb **fresh potato gnocchi**
4 large **ripe tomatoes,**
  coarsely chopped
small bunch of **basil leaves,**
  coarsely shredded
4 oz **mozzarella cheese,**
  torn into pieces
4 oz **sliced chorizo**
1–2 tablespoons **balsamic**
  vinegar
salt and **black pepper**

Heat the olive oil in a large, nonstick skillet and add the gnocchi. Pan-fry for about 8 minutes, moving frequently, until crisp and golden.

Meanwhile, toss the tomatoes with the basil leaves and torn mozzarella, season to taste, and arrange on 4 serving plates.

Add the chorizo to the skillet of gnocchi for the final 1–2 minutes of cooking, until slightly crisp and golden. Sprinkle the gnocchi and chorizo over the salads and drizzle with a little balsamic vinegar to serve.

For pan-fried gnocchi, pancetta & arugula salad,
cook the gnocchi as above, adding 4 oz chopped pancetta to the skillet for the final 2 minutes of cooking. Meanwhile, place 1 cup drained and rinsed canned chickpeas in a bowl and add 2 chopped scallions, 10 halved cherry tomatoes, 1½ tablespoons red wine vinegar, ¼ cup olive oil, and 2 tablespoons frozen chopped parsley. Season to taste and toss well. Arrange 1 (5 oz) package arugula on a large serving plate, top with the chickpea mixture, then sprinkle the gnocchi and pancetta on top and serve immediately.

beef, chile & orange stir-fry

Serves **2**
Preparation time **3 minutes**
Cooking time **7 minutes**

1 teaspoon **cornstarch**
⅔ cup **orange juice**
2 tablespoons **sweet chili sauce**
1 tablespoon **sunflower oil**
10 oz **beef strips**
1 teaspoon **prepared chopped ginger**
1 bunch of **scallions**, sliced
2 cups halved **snow peas**

Place the cornstarch in a bowl and stir in 1 tablespoon of the orange juice. Add the remaining orange juice and sweet chili sauce and stir to combine.

Heat the oil in a wok or large skillet and when hot, add the beef and ginger and stir-fry for 3–4 minutes, until browned. Add the scallions and snow peas and stir-fry for 1 minute.

Add the orange juice mixture and cook, stirring continuously, for 1–2 minutes, until the mixture thickens and coats the beef. Serve immediately.

For beef teriyaki stir-fry, mix 1 teaspoon prepared chopped ginger in a large bowl with 1 teaspoon prepared chopped garlic, 3 tablespoons dark soy sauce, 3 tablespoons mirin or dry sherry, and 2 teaspoons brown sugar. Stir in 10 oz beef strips. Heat 1 tablespoon oil in a wok or large skillet, use a slotted spoon to transfer the beef to the wok, and stir-fry for 4–5 minutes, until browned. Stir 1 teaspoon cornstarch into the remaining sauce in the bowl and add to the wok. Cook until the sauce thickens and serve immediately.

chicken, apricot & almond salad

Serves **4**
Preparation time **10 minutes**

2 cups thinly sliced **celery**
½ cup **blanched almonds**,
  coarsely chopped
3 tablespoons chopped
  parsley
¼ cup **mayonnaise**
1 lb **cooked chicken breast**,
  shredded (about **3 cups**)
12 **apricots**, halved and pitted
salt and **black pepper**

Place the celery, half the almonds, the parsley, and mayonnaise in a large bowl, season to taste, and toss to combine.

Add the chicken and apricots, stir lightly, and transfer to a serving plate. Garnish with the remaining almonds to serve.

For chicken, apricot & tomato pita pockets, dice 12 pitted apricots and toss with 3 diced, ripe tomatoes, 1 lb cooked chicken breast, shredded (about 3 cups), 3 tablespoons chopped fresh cilantro ,and a large handful of arugula. Whisk 3 tablespoons red wine vinegar with 3 tablespoons olive oil, 1 teaspoon brown sugar, and 1 teaspoon soy sauce and pour the dressing over the salad. Mix well and serve in warmed pita breads.

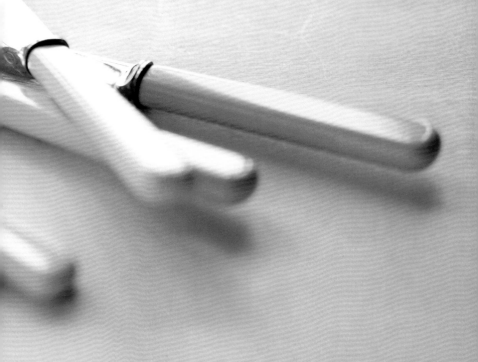

fish &
seafood

salmon & potato casseroles

Serves **2**
Preparation time **1 minute**
Cooking time **9 minutes**

1 cup **prepared cheese sauce**
½ cup **frozen peas**
1 (7½ oz) **can salmon**, drained
2 cups **store-bought mashed potatoes**
¼ cup shredded **sharp cheddar cheese**
salt and **black pepper**

Place the cheese sauce in a medium saucepan and heat gently, then stir in the peas and simmer for 3 minutes. Flake the salmon and remove any skin and bones.

Add the salmon to the saucepan, heat through, and season to taste. Divide the salmon mixture between 2 small ovenproof dishes.

Meanwhile, heat the mashed potatoes in the microwave according to package directions. Spoon the hot potatoes over the top of the fish and sprinkle with the cheese.

Place the dishes on a baking sheet and cook under a preheated hot broiler for 3–4 minutes, until golden and bubbling. Serve immediately.

For tuna & potato fish cakes, drain 1 (5 oz) can chunk light tuna in spring water and mix with 1 cup store-bought cooked mashed potatoes and 2 tablespoons chopped parsley. Season to taste and shape the mixture into 4 fish cakes, using lightly floured hands. Heat 1 tablespoon oil in a skillet and cook the fish cakes over medium to high heat for 3 minutes on each side, until browned. Serve immediately with lemon wedges and a crisp salad.

seared swordfish with chermoula

Serves **4**
Preparation time **5 minutes**
Cooking time **5 minutes**

1 (6–7 oz) package **flavored couscous**
¼ cup **raisins**
4 **swordfish steaks**, about 6 oz each
oil, for brushing
¼ cup chopped **fresh cilantro leaves**

Chermoula
1 cup **fresh cilantro**
1 cup **flat-leaf parsley**
2 teaspoons **sweet paprika**
1 teaspoon **ground cumin**
½ teaspoon **dried red pepper flakes**
¼ cup **lemon juice**
2 **garlic cloves**, peeled
¼ cup **sunflower oil**
salt and **black pepper**

Prepare the coucous according to the package directions, adding the raisins at the same time as the grains.

Meanwhile, make the chermoula by coarsely tearing up the herbs and placing them in a food processor with all the other ingredients. Season to taste and blend to a coarse paste. Smear the chermoula over both sides of the swordfish steaks.

Brush a large, ridged grill pan or heavy skillet with oil and heat over high heat. Add the swordfish and cook for 1½–2 minutes on each side, until just cooked through. Serve immediately, with the chopped cilantro tossed through the prepared couscous.

For seared swordfish with green salsa, place 1 peeled garlic clove in a food processor with 2 tablespoons capers, 2 anchovy fillets, ¼ cup chopped dill, ¼ cup chopped flat-leaf parsley, 3 tablespoons olive oil, 1 tablespoon lemon juice, and 1 teaspoon whole-grain mustard and blend until smooth. Cook the swordfish as above, without the chermoula, then remove the pan from the heat and pour in the salsa. Serve immediately with a crusty baguette and a handful of arugula.

crab & grapefruit salad

Serves **4**
Preparation time **10 minutes**

2 (6½ oz) cans **white crabmeat**
1 **pink grapefruit**, peeled and sliced
2 cups **arugula**
3 **scallions**, sliced
3 cups halved **snow peas**
salt and **black pepper**
4 **chapattis**, toasted, to serve

Dressing
3 cups **watercress** or **arugula**, tough stems removed
1 tablespoon **Dijon mustard**
2 tablespoons **olive oil**

Arrange the crabmeat, grapefruit, arugula, scallions, and snow peas on a serving plate and season to taste.

Make the dressing by placing the watercress or arugula, mustard, and oil in a food processor. Season with salt and blend until smooth.

Drizzle the dressing over the salad and serve with the toasted chapattis.

For warm shrimp & asparagus salad, cut 2 red-skinned or white round peeled potatoes into ¾ inch dice and cook in a saucepan of lightly salted boiling water for 6–7 minutes, until tender, adding 4 oz fine asparagus spears for the final 3 minutes of cooking. Mix 1 lb cooked, peeled shrimp in a salad bowl with the arugula, scallions, and snow peas. Make the dressing as above, and lightly toss into the salad with the drained potatoes and asparagus. Serve immediately.

spicy broiled sardines

Serves **2**
Preparation time **5 minutes**
Cooking time **3–5 minutes**

6 large prepared **fresh
    sardines**
1 teaspoon **prepared
    chopped garlic**
finely grated rind and juice of
    ½ **lemon**
1 teaspoon **ground cumin**
1 teaspoon **hot smoked
    paprika**
1 tablespoon **olive oil**
salt and **black pepper**

To serve
ciabatta bread, toasted
crisp green salad
lemon wedges

Use a sharp knife to make 3 slashes on each side of
the fish, cutting through the skin and flesh to the bone.
Arrange the sardines on a baking sheet.

Mix together all the remaining ingredients, season to
taste, then rub all over the fish to coat thoroughly.

Cook the sardines under a preheated hot broiler or
on a barbecue, turning once, for 3–5 minutes or until
cooked through. Serve with toasted ciabatta, a crisp
green salad, and lemon wedges.

For mackerel with warm potato & mustard salad,
thinly slice 8 oz new potatoes and cook in a saucepan
of lightly salted boiling water with 1½ halved, trimmed
green beans for 4–5 minutes, until tender. Meanwhile,
season 4 mackerel fillets and heat 1 tablespoon olive
oil in a large skillet. When the oil is hot, cook the fish,
skin side down, for 2–3 minutes, then turn over and
cook for an additional minute. Mix 1 tablespoon capers
with ¼ cup prepared honey and mustard salad dressing
and pour over the drained potatoes and beans. Divide
between 2 plates and serve the mackerel on top.

crispy coconut shrimp

Serves **4**
Preparation time **6 minutes**
Cooking time **3–4 minutes**

¼ cup **dried bread crumbs**
1 cup **dried coconut**
¼ cup **cornstarch**
1 extra-large **egg white**
⅔ cup **sunflower oil**
8 oz **raw, peeled
  jumbo shrimp**
salt and **black pepper**

To serve
lime wedges
sweet chili dipping sauce

Place the bread crumbs and coconut in a food processor and pulse together briefly to break up the coconut a little. Transfer to a shallow bowl.

Season the cornstarch with salt and freshly ground black pepper and place on a plate. Lightly beat the egg white in a shallow bowl.

Heat the oil in a deep fryer or deep, heavy saucepan to 350˚F, or until a cube of bread browns in 15 seconds.

Meanwhile, toss the shrimp, a few at a time, in the cornstarch and shake off the excess. Dip them in the egg white to cover, then roll in the coconut mixture to make an even coating. Spread out on a large plate or baking sheet.

Cook the shrimp in the hot oil for 3–4 minutes, lightly shaking to separate them, until golden brown. Remove them with a slotted spoon and drain on paper towels. Serve with lime wedges and sweet chili dipping sauce.

For crispy sesame shrimp toasts, cut 4 slices of slightly stale white bread into 4 triangles each. Place 12 oz raw, peeled jumbo shrimp in a food processor with 1 teaspoon prepared chopped ginger, ½ teaspoon salt, 2 chopped scallions, 1 tablespoon cornstarch, 1 teaspoon sesame oil, and 1 egg white. Blend to a paste, spread thickly on the bread, then sprinkle with sesame seeds. Heat the oil as above and cook the toasts, a few at a time, shrimp side down, for about 1 minute, until golden. Turn over and cook for an additional 1–2 minutes. Remove with a slotted spoon and drain on paper towels. Serve hot.

vegetable broth with sea bass

Serves **4**
Preparation time **4 minutes**
Cooking time **6–7 minutes**

3 cups good-quality **chicken**
   or **vegetable stock**
2 tablespoons **olive oil**
4 **sea bass fillets**, about
   7 oz each
1 **fennel bulb**, trimmed and
   cut into 8 wedges
12 **fine asparagus spears**
1 cup **frozen peas**, thawed
1 cup **shelled fava beans**
small handful of **mint**
   leaves, torn
small handful of **basil**
   leaves, torn
salt and **black pepper**
crusty bread, to serve

Bring the stock to a boil in a large saucepan. Heat the oil in a large, heavy skillet.

Season the sea bass fillets and cook, skin side down, in the skillet for 3–4 minutes, until the skin is crispy. Turn over and cook for 1 minute on the other side.

Meanwhile, cook the fennel in the simmering stock for 3 minutes, or until it is just starting to become tender. Add the asparagus, peas, and fava beans to the pan and cook for an additional 1–2 minutes. Season to taste.

Divide the vegetable broth among 4 bowls and sprinkle with the herbs. Top each portion with a sea bass fillet and serve immediately.

For Thai broth with shrimp, bring 3 cups fish stock to a boil in a large saucepan with 1 tablespoon lemon grass paste, 2 tablespoons prepared chopped ginger, ½ teaspoon dried red pepper flakes, and 2 kaffir lime leaves and simmer for 3 minutes. Season to taste, add 1 lb raw, peeled jumbo shrimp and poach gently for 2–3 minutes, then add 2 cups sugar snap peas and 5 oz store-bought, cooked rice noodles and cook for an additonal 1 minute. Serve immediately.

haddock on toast

Serves **4**
Preparation time **2 minutes**
Cooking time **7–8 minutes**

4 **smoked haddock fillets**,
   about 5 oz each
1 ¼ cups **prepared
   cheese sauce**
1 teaspoon **English mustard**
2 **egg yolks**
2 teaspoons **Worcestershire
   sauce**
2 tablespoons chopped
   flat-leaf parsley
¼ cup **sharp cheddar cheese**

To serve
prepared mashed potatoes
frozen peas

Place the haddock in a single layer in a deep skillet
with a lid and pour enough boiling water over it to cover.
Bring to a boil, cover, and simmer gently for 2 minutes,
until half cooked. Carefully transfer the fish fillets to a
shallow ovenproof dish and keep warm.

Meanwhile, place the cheese sauce in a small
saucepan and heat through. Remove from the heat
and stir in the mustard, egg yolks, Worcestershire
sauce, and parsley.

Top the fish with the mixture, sprinkle with the cheddar
cheese, and cook under a preheated hot broiler for
3-4 minutes, until bubbling and golden. Serve at once
with mashed potatoes and peas.

For smoked haddock, spinach & lima bean salad,
put 1 lb smoked haddock in a saucepan and pour
enough boiling water over it to just cover. Cook for
4–5 minutes, until cooked through, drain, and let cool
slightly. Meanwhile, drain 1 (15 oz) can lima beans
and put in a bowl with 4 cups baby spinach, 3 sliced
scallions, and 4 cooked beets, cut into wedges.
Flake the fish, removing any skin and bones, and
add to the bowl. Whisk 1 teaspoon Dijon mustard
with 1 teaspoon white wine vinegar, 3 tablespoons
sour cream, 3 tablespoons light olive oil, and
1 tablespoon chopped dill. Season to taste,
pour the dressing over the salad, and gently toss
together. Serve immediately.

broiled cod with tapenade

Serves **4**
Preparation time **2 minutes**
Cooking time **8 minutes**

4 chunky **cod fillets**, about
    6 oz each
oil, for brushing
salt and **black pepper**
tomato and red onion salad,
    to serve

Dressing
½ cup **pitted ripe**
    black olives
2 **anchovy fillets in oil**,
    drained
2 teaspoons **capers in brine**,
    drained and rinsed
1 **garlic clove**, peeled
1 teaspoon **thyme leaves**
¼ cup **light olive oil**
1 tablespoon **red wine**
    vinegar

Brush the cod fillets with a little oil and season to taste. Cook under a preheated hot broiler for 4 minutes on each side, until cooked through.

Meanwhile, place the olives, anchovies, capers, garlic, and thyme in a food processor and pulse until coarsely chopped. Stir in the oil and vinegar.

Transfer the fish to serving plates and spoon the tapenade dressing on top. Serve immediately with a tomato and red onion salad.

For baked cod with a herb & anchovy crust, preheat the oven to 400°F. Mix 1 cup whole-wheat bread crumbs with 2 tablespoons chopped parsley, the grated rind of ½ lemon, and 1 (2 oz) can anchovy fillets in oil, drained and chopped. Place 4 cod fillets, skin side down, on a baking sheet and spoon over the crumb topping. Cook in the preheated oven for 7–8 minutes, until the topping is browned and the cod cooked through. Serve with a crisp salad.

peppercorn-crusted tuna steaks

Serves **4**
Preparation time **3 minutes**
Cooking time **6–7 minutes**

4 **tuna steaks**, about 5 oz
   each
2 teaspoons **mixed**
   peppercorns, crushed
4 cups **sugar snap peas**
1 teaspoon **sesame oil**
2 teaspoons **sesame seeds,**
   lightly toasted
store-bought cooked rice
   noodles, to serve

Dressing
2 tablespoons **light soy sauce**
¼ cup **mirin**
1 teaspoon **sugar**
1 teaspoon **wasabi paste**

Season the tuna steaks all over with the crushed peppercorns. Heat a ridged grill pan over medium-high heat and grill the tuna steaks for 2 minutes on each side, until browned on the outside but still pink in the middle. Remove from the pan and let rest.

Drizzle the sugar snap peas with the sesame oil and steam over a saucepan of gently simmering water for 2–3 minutes or until tender.

Place all the dressing ingredients in a screw-top jar and shake vigorously until well combined.

Divide the sugar snap peas among 4 serving plates, then cut the tuna steaks in half diagonally and arrange on the peas. Drizzle with the dressing and sprinkle with the sesame seeds. Serve immediately with rice noodles.

mussels with cider & herb broth

Serves **4**
Preparation time **2 minutes**
Cooking time **8 minutes**

1 tablespoon **butter**
1 **prepared chopped onion**
1 teaspoon **prepared
chopped garlic**
4 lb **prepared mussels**
⅔ cup **cider**
⅔ cup **crème fraîche** or
heavy cream
2 tablespoons chopped
tarragon
2 tablespoons chopped
flat-leaf parsley
crusty bread, to serve

Melt the butter in a large saucepan and cook the onion and garlic for 2–3 minutes. Meanwhile, discard any mussels that are open and do not close when tapped.

Add the cider and mussels to the pan and cover with a lid. Cook over high heat for 3–4 minutes, shaking the pan from time to time, until all the mussels have opened.

Discard any mussels which have not opened, then stir in the crème fraîche or heavy cream and herbs and heat through. Serve immediately with crusty bread.

For rustic seafood soup, heat 1 tablespoon olive oil in a large saucepan and cook 1 prepared chopped onion and 1 teaspoon prepared chopped garlic for 2 minutes, until softened. Stir in ⅔ cup white wine, 1 (14½ oz) can diced tomatoes, 2 cups boiling fish stock, and a sprig of thyme. Boil for 4 minutes, then stir in 8 oz diced cod fillet, 8 oz raw, peeled jumbo shrimp, and 8 oz store-bought prepared mussels. Simmer for 3–4 minutes, until the shrimp have turned pink and the mussels have opened. Discard any mussels that do not open, season to taste, and serve immediately with crusty bread.

shrimp, mango & avocado salad

Serves **4**
Preparation time **10 minutes**

1 large **mango**, peeled
and pitted
1 ripe **avocado**, peeled
and pitted
2 large **romaine lettuce**
16 large **cooked, peeled
jumbo shrimp**

Dressing
juice of 2 **limes**
1 teaspoon **brown sugar**
2 tablespoons **vegetable oil**
½ **fresh red chile**, seeded
and finely chopped

Cut the mango and avocado into ¾ inch pieces and
separate the lettuce into leaves. Arrange the lettuce,
mango, avocado, and shrimp on a serving plate.

Make the dressing by whisking all the ingredients
together. Drizzle the dressing over the salad, toss
carefully to mix, and serve immediately.

For creamy Marie Rose sauce, a more luxurious
dressing for this salad, mix 3 tablespoons mayonnaise
with 2 tablespoons heavy cream, 2 teaspoons ketchup,
1 ½ teaspoons Worcestershire sauce, 2–3 drops
Tabasco sauce, 1 tablespoon lemon juice, and
1 tablespoon brandy. Season to taste with salt and
black pepper and drizzle the dressing over the salad.

japanese-style crispy fish goujons

Serves **2**
Preparation time **4 minutes**
Cooking time **6 minutes**

⅔ cup **sunflower oil**
8 oz **cod** or **haddock fillets**
3 tablespoons **cornstarch**
1 **egg**, beaten
1 cup **dried panko**
   (Japanese bread crumbs)
salt and **black pepper**
lemon wedges, to serve

Wasabi mayonnaise
¼ cup **mayonnaise**
½ teaspoon **wasabi paste**

Cut the fish into ½ inch strips and season to taste. Place the cornstarch, egg, and bread crumbs in 3 separate shallow bowls. Dip the fish pieces first in the cornstarch, then in the egg, and finally in the bread crumbs to coat them and spread out on a large plate or baking sheet.

Meanwhile, heat the oil in a deep fryer or deep, heavy saucepan to 350°F, or until a cube of bread browns in 15 seconds.

Cook the fish in the hot oil for 3–4 minutes, until golden brown, then remove with a slotted spoon and drain on paper towels. Mix the mayonnaise with the wasabi. Serve the crispy fish immediately with the spicy mayonnaise and some lemon wedges.

For fish goujon sandwiches, prepare and cook the fish as above. Meanwhile, split 2 large soft bread rolls and spread with a little softened butter. Place the fish goujons on the bottom halves and top each with 1–2 tablespoons prepared tartar sauce and a handful of arugula leaves. Replace the tops of the rolls and serve immediately with lemon wedges.

spiced mackerel fillets

Serves **4**
Preparation time **4 minutes**
Cooking time **5–6 minutes**

2 tablespoons **olive oil**
1 tablespoon **smoked paprika**
1 teaspoon **cayenne pepper**
8 **mackerel fillets**
2 **limes**, quartered
salt and **black pepper**
arugula salad, to serve

Mix the oil with the paprika and cayenne and season to taste. Make 3 shallow cuts in the skin of each mackerel fillet and brush all over with the spiced oil.

Cook the lime quarters with the mackerel fillets on a hot barbecue grill or under a preheated hot broiler, skin side first, for 4–5 minutes, until the skin is crispy and the limes are charred.

Turn the fish over and cook for an additional minute on the other side. Serve with an arugula salad.

For black pepper & bay mackerel, mix together 4 finely shredded bay leaves, 1 crushed garlic clove, ½ teaspoon freshly ground black pepper, a pinch of salt, and ¼ cup olive oil. Rub the marinade over and into the cavities of 4 whole, prepared mackerel. Cook on a hot barbecue or under a preheated hot broiler for 3–4 minutes on each side. Serve with a tomato salad.

cod tacos with lime & cilantro

Serves **4**
Preparation time **4 minutes**
Cooking time **6 minutes**

1 ¼ lb **cod** or **haddock fillets,**
   cut into 1 inch cubes
2 tablespoons **Cajun**
   seasoning
8 **taco shells**
1 tablespoon **peanut oil**
2 tablespoons **lime juice**
1 small **butterhead lettuce,**
   shredded
¼ cup chopped **fresh cilantro**
1 cup **prepared guacamole**
1 cup **prepared fresh**
   tomato salsa

Preheat the oven to 350°F. Place the fish in a large bowl and sprinkle with the Cajun seasoning. Gently shake the bowl to coat the fish pieces in the seasoning.

Arrange the taco shells upright in an ovenproof dish and warm in the preheated oven for 5 minutes.

Meanwhile, heat the oil in a large skillet and cook the fish pieces for 2–3 minutes on each side, until cooked through. Carefully transfer the fish to a bowl and drizzle with the lime juice.

Fill the taco shells with the lettuce and top with the fish. Sprinkle the cilantro on top and serve immediately with the tomato salsa and guacamole.

For Cajun cod tortillas with lime crème fraîche,

sprinkle 1 tablespoon Cajun seasoning over 4 cod fillets, about 6 oz each. Melt 2 tablespoons butter in a skillet and cook the fish for 3–4 minutes each side, until cooked through. Meanwhile, mix ½ cup crème fraîche or Greek yogurt with 1 tablespoon lime juice and 2 tablespoons chopped fresh cilantro. Serve the fish with warmed soft flour tortillas, the crème fraîche, and a crisp salad.

mixed seafood with peppercorns

Serves **4**
Preparation time **5 minutes**
Cooking time **5 minutes**

3 tablespoons **peanut oil**
2 **garlic cloves**, finely chopped
4 **scallops**, quartered
6 **crab sticks**, halved
8 oz **cooked, peeled
  jumbo shrimp**
1 tablespoon **Thai fish sauce**
1 tablespoon **oyster sauce**
1 tablespoon **light soy sauce**
1 teaspoon **brown sugar**
2 tablespoons **fresh green
  peppercorns**
cooked rice, to serve

Heat the oil in a wok or large skillet over high heat until the oil starts to shimmer. Add the garlic and stir-fry for a few seconds, then add the scallops and stir-fry for 1 minute, until browned.

Add the crab sticks, shrimp, fish sauce, oyster sauce, soy sauce, sugar, and peppercorns, in that order, giving the dish a quick stir between each addition.

Cook for an additional 1 minute, until all the fish is heated through and well coated in the sauce. Serve with rice.

For coconut rice, to serve as an accompaniment, heat 1 tablespoon peanut oil in a wok or large skillet and add ⅓ cup coconut milk. Bring to a boil with 1 teaspoon Thai fish sauce and stir in 2 cups store-bought cooked rice. Heat through, season to taste, add a squeeze of lime juice, and serve with the seafood.

swordfish with sage pangritata

Serves **4**
Preparation time **2 minutes**
Cooking time **8 minutes**

2½ cups **trimmed green
 beans**
⅓ cup **extra virgin olive oil**,
 plus extra for drizzling
1 tablespoon **prepared
 chopped garlic**
2 tablespoons chopped **sage
 leaves**
3 cups **fresh white
 bread crumbs**
finely grated rind and juice of
 1 **lemon**
4 **swordfish steaks**, about
 7 oz each
salt and **black pepper**

Cook the beans in a saucepan of lightly salted boiling water for 3 minutes, until just tender.

Meanwhile, heat ¼ cup of the oil in a skillet and cook the garlic, sage, bread crumbs, and lemon rind, stirring constantly, for 5 minutes, until crisp and golden. Drain the pangritata thoroughly on paper towels.

Heat a ridged grill pan until hot. Brush the swordfish with the remaining oil, season to taste, and sear in the ridged grill pan for 1½ minutes on each side.

Season the beans to taste and toss with a little of the lemon juice and a drizzle of oil.

Transfer the swordfish to 4 serving plates, drizzle with the remaining lemon juice, and top with the pangritata. Serve with the beans.

For swordfish with bacon pangritata and creamy leeks, cook 3 cups chopped leeks in a saucepan of lightly salted boiling water for 3 minutes. Make the pangritata as above, adding 3 finely chopped bacon slices, and drain on paper towels. Toss the drained leeks with 1 cup crème fraîche or Greek yogurt mixed with ½ teaspoon Dijon mustard and season to taste. Cook the swordfish as above and serve on a bed of creamy leeks, topped with the bacon pangritata.

vegetables

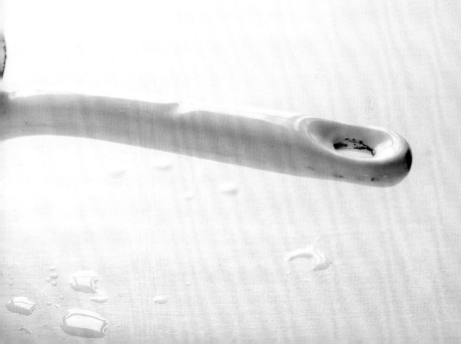

caramelized onion & brie tarts

Serves **4**
Preparation time **2 minutes**
Cooking time **7–8 minutes**

8 **store-bought pie crusts**,
   about 3½ inches
½ cup **onion relish**
4 oz **Brie cheese**,
   cut into 8 slices
thyme sprigs, to garnish

Preheat the oven to 350°F. Place the pie crusts on a baking sheet and spread 1 tablespoon of relish in the bottom of each. Top with the Brie.

Cook in the preheated oven for 7–8 minutes, until the cheese melts. Garnish with thyme sprigs and serve hot.

For creamy roasted pepper tarts, beat ½ cup light garlic and herb cream cheese with 1 egg and ¼ cup grated Parmesan cheese. Spoon the mixture into 8 individual pie crusts on a baking sheet. Top with ½ cup chopped roasted red peppers and cook in a preheated oven at 375°F for 8 minutes. Serve with salad greens.

paneer, pea & spinach curry

Serves **4**
Preparation time **2 minutes**
Cooking time **8 minutes**

2 tablespoons **peanut oil**
1 **prepared chopped onion**
1 teaspoon **prepared
   chopped garlic**
2 teaspoons **prepared
   chopped ginger**
8 oz **paneer cheese**
2 tablespoons **medium curry
   powder**
1¾ cup **coconut milk**
2 cups **frozen peas**
1 (6 oz) package
   baby spinach
salt and **black pepper**
naans, to serve

Heat the oil in a large saucepan and cook the onion, garlic, and ginger over low heat for 2–3 minutes. Meanwhile, cut the paneer into ¾ inch cubes.

Add the curry powder and cook for 1 minute, then stir in the paneer. Stir-fry for an additional minute.

Pour the coconut milk over the paneer and add the peas. Cover and simmer for 4 minutes, until the peas are tender. Stir in the spinach and cook for a few minutes, until the spinach has wilted. Season to taste and serve immediately with naans.

For tandoori paneer & mushroom kebabs, mix ¼ cup plain yogurt with 2 tablespoons tandoori curry paste and 1 tablespoon lemon juice. Stir in the paneer cubes and 16 button mushrooms to coat. Thread onto 4 metal skewers and cook under a preheated hot broiler or barbecue on a grill for 8 minutes, turning occasionally and brushing with any remaining yogurt mixture. Serve with salad and naans.

mushrooms with mascarpone

Serves **4**
Preparation time **2 minutes**
Cooking time **8 minutes**

2 tablespoons **butter**
1 teaspoon **prepared chopped garlic**
7 cups **sliced mushrooms** (about 1 lb)
2 tablespoons **marsala wine** or **sherry**
3 tablespoons **mascarpone cheese**
2 tablespoons coarsely chopped **tarragon**
salt and **black pepper**
crusty bread, to serve

Melt the butter in a large skillet. When foaming, add the garlic and mushrooms and cook over high heat for 5 minutes, stirring occasionally, until the mushrooms are lightly browned.

Stir in the marsala or sherry and simmer for 2 minutes. Add the mascarpone and stir until melted into the sauce, then stir in the tarragon. Season to taste and serve immediately with crusty bread.

For mushroom stroganoff, cook 7 cups sliced mushrooms (about 1 lb) in 2 tablespoons butter as above until lightly browned. Stir in 1 teaspoon paprika and 1 tablespoon brandy and cook for 1 minute. Add 1¼ cups sour cream, simmer for 2 minutes then season to taste and stir in 2 tablespoons chopped parsley. Serve immediately with cooked rice.

mixed vegetable hash

Serves **2**
Preparation time **2 minutes**
Cooking time **8 minutes**

2 cups chopped **curly kale**
1 tablespoon **sunflower oil**
1 small **prepared
chopped onion**
1 tablespoon **whole-grain
mustard**
2 cups **prepared mixed
mashed potoatoes
and carrots** or **mashed
potatoes**
salt and **black pepper**

Cook the kale in a large saucepan of lightly salted boiling water for 3 minutes. Meanwhile, heat the oil in a nonstick skillet and cook the onion for 2 minutes, until softened.

Stir the mustard into the mashed vegetables and add to the skillet. Add the drained kale, season to taste, and mix well. Cook over medium heat for 3 minutes on one side until browned, then flip the mixture over and cook for an additional 2 minutes, until piping hot. Serve immediately.

For minted pea & potato hash, cook 1 ⅓ cups frozen peas according to package directions, then drain and roughly mash with a potato masher. Stir 2 cups prepared mashed potatoes into the peas with 2 tablespoons freshly chopped mint and season to taste. Meanwhile, heat 1 tablespoon oil in a nonstick skillet and add the potato and pea mixture. Cook for 3 minutes each side, until browned. Serve immediately.

garlicky broccoli raab

Serves **4**
Preparation time **5 minutes**
Cooking time **5 minutes**

2 tablespoons **peanut oil**

3 **garlic cloves**, sliced

1 teaspoon **salt**

1 lb **broccoli raab**, trimmed
   and cut into 2 inch pieces

2 tablespoons **Chinese rice
   wine** or **dry sherry**

⅔ cup **water**

1 teaspoon **sesame oil**

Heat the oil in a wok or large skillet over high heat until the oil starts to shimmer. Add the garlic and salt and stir-fry for 15 seconds, then add the broccoli raab and stir-fry for 1 minute.

Add the rice wine and measured water and stir-fry for 2–3 minutes, until the broccoli raab is tender and most of the liquid has evaporated.

Stir in the sesame oil and serve immediately.

For bok choy with water chestnuts & garlic, follow the recipe above, replacing the broccoli raab with 1 lb bok choy, cut into 2 inch lengths, and 4 sliced canned water chestnuts.

broccoli & cauliflower gratin

Serves **4**
Preparation time **2 minutes**
Cooking time **7–8 minutes**

4 cups small **cauliflower
florets**
4 cups small **broccoli florets**
1½ cups **prepared
cheese sauce**
8 **sun-dried tomatoes**,
drained and coarsely
chopped
½ cup shredded **sharp
cheddar cheese**
salt

Cook the cauliflower in a large saucepan of lightly salted boiling water for 2 minutes, then add the broccoli and cook for an additional 3 minutes, until the vegetables are just tender. Drain well.

Meanwhile, place the sauce in a medium saucepan and cook over moderate heat, stirring occasionally, until simmering. Stir in the sun-dried tomatoes, cauliflower, and broccoli and mix together.

Transfer to a shallow ovenproof dish, sprinkle with the shredded cheese, and cook under a preheated hot broiler for 2–3 minutes, until the cheese has melted.

For stir-fried broccoli with oyster sauce, cook 1 lb baby broccoli in a saucepan of lightly salted boiling water for 3–4 minutes. Plunge into cold water, then drain well. Meanwhile, blend 2 teaspoons cornstarch with 2 tablespoons water in a small bowl. Heat 1 tablespoon sunflower oil in a wok or large skillet and add 1 teaspoon prepared chopped garlic and the broccoli and stir-fry for 1 minute. Add ¼ cup oyster sauce, cook for 1 minute, then stir in the blended cornstarch. When the sauce starts to thicken, stir in ½ teaspoon sesame oil. Serve with cooked rice.

spinach, potato & ricotta frittata

Serves **4**
Preparation time **1 minute**
Cooking time **7–9 minutes**

8 oz **new potatoes**,
  thinly sliced
1 tablespoon **olive oil**
3½ cups **baby spinach**
6 **eggs**
2 tablespoons snipped **chives**
½ cup **ricotta cheese**
salt and **black pepper**

Cook the potatoes in a saucepan of lightly salted boiling water for 2–3 minutes, until just tender. Meanwhile, heat the oil in an 11 inch ovenproof skillet, add the spinach, and cook for 1–2 minutes, until wilted.

Beat the eggs in a small bowl with the chives and season to taste. Drain the potatoes and stir into the skillet with the spinach, then add the eggs and stir briefly. Cook, without stirring, over medium heat for 3–4 minutes, until almost set.

Arrange the ricotta over the frittata and continue to cook under a preheated hot broiler for 2 minutes, until golden. Cut into wedges and serve immediately.

For corn kernels & roasted pepper frittata, heat 1 tablespoon olive oil in a skillet as above, then stir in 1 cup chopped roasted red peppers and 1¼ cups canned corn kernels and cook for 1 minute. Beat 6 eggs with 2 tablespoons chopped parsley and season to taste. Pour into the skillet and cook as above, then sprinkle with 1 cup shredded cheddar cheese and broil until browned.

vegetarian club sandwich

Serves **1**
Preparation time **7 minutes**
Cooking time **2–3 minutes**

3 slices of **whole-grain bread**
1 **carrot**, shredded
2 tablespoons **mayonnaise**
2 tablespoons **prepared hummus**
1 **tomato**, thickly sliced
large handful of **arugula**
freshly ground black pepper

Lightly toast the bread in a toaster or under a preheated hot broiler. Meanwhile, mix the shredded carrot with the mayonnaise and season with black pepper.

Spread the hummus on 1 slice of the toast and top with half the tomato slices and arugula.

Place a second slice of toast on top and spoon the carrot mixture on top. Top with the remaining tomato and arugula. Place the remaining slice of toast on top and press down gently. Cut the sandwich in half or quarters and secure with toothpicks. Serve immediately.

For avocado, cheese & sprout club sandwich, lightly toast 3 slices of whole-grain bread. Spread 2 slices of the bread with 1 tablespoon mayonnaise and top each with a slice of cheese, a little alfafa sprouts, and ¼ diced avocado. Place one slice on top of the other, then top with the remaining slice of toast. Serve as above.

herbed lima bean salad

Serves **4**
Preparation time **10 minutes**

2 (15 oz) **cans lima beans**,
  rinsed and drained
1 oz **prosciutto**, chopped
4 **ripe tomatoes**, sliced
1 **mild Spanish onion**, sliced

Dressing
⅓ cup chopped **flat-leaf
  parsley**
⅓ cup chopped **mint**
finely grated rind and juice of
  2 **lemons**
2 tablespoons **prepared
  chopped garlic**
1 tablespoon **olive oil**
2 teaspoons **cider vinegar**
salt and **black pepper**

Arrange the beans and ham in a serving dish with the sliced tomatoes and onion.

Make the dressing by whisking together all the ingredients. Season to taste and drizzle it over the salad.

For herbed chickpea & tuna salad, use 3 cups drained, canned chickpeas and 1 (5 oz) can tuna instead of the lima beans and ham. Drain the tuna and toss with the chickpeas, then add the tomatoes and onion and divide among 4 serving dishes. Make the dressing as above and pour it over the salad.

tofu with black bean & cashews

Serves **2**
Preparation time **2 minutes**
Cooking time **8 minutes**

1 tablespoon **sunflower oil**
5 oz **firm tofu**, cut into ¾ inch
  cubes (about ⅔ cup)
1 teaspoon **prepared**
  chopped ginger
1 (12 oz) package
  stir-fry vegetables with
  mixed bell peppers
½ cup **raw cashew nuts**
2 tablespoons **oyster sauce**
3 tablespoons **black bean**
  sauce
cooked noodles, to serve

Heat the oil in a wok or large skillet until starting to smoke, add the tofu, and stir-fry over high heat for 2 minutes, until browned. Remove from the wok and keep warm.

Add the ginger, prepared vegetables, and cashew nuts to the wok and stir-fry for 5 minutes, or according to package directions, until the vegetables are tender and the nuts are lightly browned.

Stir in the oyster sauce and black bean sauce and return the tofu to the wok. Cook for 1 minute, then serve immediately with noodles.

For crispy tofu with ginger, chile & sugar snaps, toss 8 oz diced tofu (about 1 cup) in a bowl with 1 tablespoon rice flour. Meanwhile, heat 1 tablespoon sunflower oil in a wok or nonstick skillet, add the tofu, and cook for 3–4 minutes, turning occasionally, until crisp. Remove from the wok. Add a little more oil to the wok, add 1 tablespoon prepared chopped ginger and 2 cups sugar snaps, and stir-fry for 2–3 minutes. Mix 2 tablespoons mirin with 2 tablespoons sweet chili sauce and 1 teaspoon sesame oil and add to the wok. Remove from the heat and stir in the tofu. Serve immediately with noodles.

baby vegetables with pesto

Serves **4**
Preparation time **2 minutes**
Cooking time **8 minutes**

8–12 **baby zucchini**, halved
    lengthwise
2–4 **baby leeks**, halved
    lengthwise
12–16 **baby carrot**s, halved
    lengthwise
4 oz trimmed **asparagus**
    spears
2 tablespoons **olive oil**
2 tablespoons **lemon juice**
¼ cup **fresh pesto sauce**
salt and **black pepper**
focaccia bread, to serve

Place all the vegetables in a large bowl and add the oil. Season to taste and stir gently to coat.

Heat a large, ridged grill pan over high heat, add half the vegetables, and cook for about 2 minutes on each side, until lightly charred. Remove from the pan and keep warm while you cook the remaining vegetables in the same way.

Divide the vegetables among 4 serving plates, drizzle with the lemon juice, then spoon the pesto over them. Serve immediately with focaccia.

For pea & pesto soup, place 3 cups boiling vegetable stock in a large saucepan. Add 3 cups frozen peas and simmer for 5 minutes, until tender. Using a handheld immersion blender or a food processor, blend the soup until smooth. Return to the pan and stir in 2 tablespoons crème fraîche or heavy cream and 2 tablespoons fresh pesto sauce. Heat through, season to taste, and serve immediately with crusty bread.

moroccan vegetable couscous

Serves **4**
Preparation time **5 minutes**
Cooking time **5 minutes**

1 tablespoon **harissa paste,**
   plus extra to serve
finely grated rind and juice of
   1 lemon
1 cup **couscous**
1¼ cups **boiling water**
1 tablespoon **olive oil**
1 lb **frozen roasted**
   Mediterranean vegetables,
   such as eggplant, zucchini,
   bell peppers, and onions
2 **preserved lemons,** rinsed
1 (15 oz) **can chickpeas,**
   drained and rinsed
small bunch of **fresh cilantro,**
   coarsely chopped
salt and **black pepper**
plain yogurt, to serve

Put the harissa and lemon rind and juice in a large heatproof bowl and add the couscous and boiling water. Stir, cover, and let stand for 5 minutes. Season to taste and fluff with a fork.

Meanwhile, heat the oil in a large skillet, add the vegetables, and stir-fry over moderate heat for 3–4 minutes. Cut the preserved lemons into quarters, remove the flesh and discard, then coarsely chop the skin.

Stir the vegetables and preserved lemon skin into the couscous with the chickpeas and cilantro. Season to taste and serve warm with a spoonful of yogurt and a drizzle of harissa.

For curried vegetable couscous, place 2 teaspoons mild curry paste in a large bowl with ¼ cup orange juice and stir together. Add the couscous and ⅓ cup dried cranberries and stir well. Add the boiling water and let soak as above. Cook the vegetables as above and stir into the couscous with the chickpeas and cilantro. Serve with a spoonful of mango chutney.

creamy leek & lima bean gratin

Serves **4**
Preparation time **2 minutes**
Cooking time **7–8 minutes**

1 tablespoon **butter**
2 **leeks**, cut into 1 inch pieces
2 (15 oz) **cans lima beans**,
   drained and rinsed
¾ cup **light cream cheese**
   with garlic and herbs
2 tablespoons **milk**
¼ cup **fresh white**
   bread crumbs
2 tablespoons **freshly grated**
   Parmesan cheese
salt and **black pepper**

Melt the butter in a medium saucepan, add the leeks, and cook for 3–4 minutes, until softened. Stir in the lima beans, cream cheese, and milk and cook for 2 minutes, until the lima beans are heated through and the sauce is bubbling. Season to taste.

Meanwhile, mix together the bread crumbs and Parmesan cheese.

Transfer the bean mixture to a warmed ovenproof dish, sprinkle with the bread crumbs and cheese, and cook under a preheated hot broiler for 2 minutes or until the topping is browned. Serve immediately.

For cheesy baby leeks, heat 1 tablespoon olive oil in a large skillet, add 16 trimmed baby leeks, season to taste, and cook for 4 minutes, until starting to brown. Add 1 cup heavy cream and cook, stirring, until bubbling. Transfer to a warmed ovenproof dish and sprinkle with ¾ cup shredded Gruyère or Swiss cheese. Cook under a preheated hot broiler for 3–4 minutes, until browned. Serve with crusty bread.

ricotta-stuffed mushrooms

Serves **2**
Preparation time **1 minute**
Cooking time **8–9 minutes**

4 large **flat cremeni** or
   portabello mushrooms
2 tablespoons **garlic-infused
   olive oil**
salt and **black pepper**
arugula salad, to serve

Filling
1 cup **ricotta cheese**
12 large **basil leaves**,
   coarsely chopped
finely grated rind of 1 **lemon**
¼ cup grated **Parmesan
   cheese**
3 tablespoons **pine nuts**

Remove the stems from the mushrooms and brush all over with the oil. Season to taste and place on a baking sheet, skin side up. Cook under a preheated hot broiler for 5 minutes.

Meanwhile, mix all the filling ingredients in a bowl and season to taste. Turn the mushrooms over and pile the filling into the cavities, pressing it down.

Cook for an additional 3–4 minutes, until the filling is browned and the mushrooms are cooked through. Serve immediately with an arugula salad.

For mushroom & ricotta frittata, heat 1 tablespoon olive oil in an 8 inch ovenproof skillet, add 2 cups sliced mushrooms and 1 teaspoon prepared chopped garlic, and cook for 3–4 minutes. Meanwhile, beat 4 eggs with 1 tablespoon chopped parsley and season to taste. Add to the skillet, stir briefly, and cook without stirring over medium heat for 3–4 minutes, until almost set. Sprinkle with ¼ cup ricotta cheese and ¼ cup grated Parmesan cheese and cook under a preheated hot broiler for 3 minutes, until browned and set. Serve with a green salad.

sweet treats

salted caramel brownies

Serves **4**
Preparation time **3 minutes**
Cooking time **7 minutes**

4 **prepared chocolate
brownies**
4 scoops of **vanilla ice cream**

Salted caramel sauce
1 stick **unsalted butter**
⅓ cup firmly packed
brown sugar
⅓ cup **light corn syrup**
1 teaspoon **vanilla extract**
⅔ cup **heavy cream**
½ teaspoon **coarse sea salt**

Make the sauce by placing the butter, sugar, light corn syrup, and vanilla in a saucepan. Bring to a boil over medium heat, stirring continuously.

Add the cream and salt and boil for 5 minutes, stirring occasionally, until thickened. Remove from the heat.

Divide the chocolate brownies among 4 bowls and top each with a scoop of ice cream. Pour over the salted caramel sauce and serve immediately.

For banana & salted caramel sundaes, make the salted caramel sauce as above. Meanwhile, coarsely chop 2 chocolate muffins and slice 4 bananas. Divide half the muffin and banana pieces among 4 sundae glasses, then top each portion with a scoop of vanilla ice cream and a drizzle of sauce. Repeat the layers, ending with a drizzle of sauce. Serve immediately.

frozen blueberry yogurt

Serves **4–6**
Preparation time **8 minutes**

2½ cups **frozen blueberries**
2 tablespoons **confectioners'
sugar**
1 tablespoon **lemon juice**
2 cups **plain yogurt**
4 **lemon shortbread cookies**,
to serve

Place the frozen blueberries in a food processor with the confectioners' sugar and lemon juice and blend until coarsely chopped. Add the yogurt and pulse until fairly smooth, scraping down the sides of the bowl from time to time.

Divide the mixture among 4 glass dishes and serve with the lemon shortbread cookies.

For frozen raspberry & vanilla yogurt, place 1½ cups frozen raspberries and 2 tablespoons confectioners' sugar in a food processor and blend until coarsely chopped. Add 2 cups vanilla-flavored yogurt and pulse until fairly smooth. Serve immediately.

pan-fried apples with calvados

Serves **2**
Preparation time **2 minutes**
Cooking time **8 minutes**

2 **Pippin** or **other red-skinned sweet apples**, cored and cut into wedges
¼ cup **granulated sugar**
2 tablespoons **unsalted butter**
2 tablespoons **Calvados** or **other apple brandy**

To serve
crème fraîche or **Greek yogurt**
ground cinnamon

Toss the apples and sugar together in a bowl. Melt the butter over low heat in a skillet, add the apples, and cook gently for 5 minutes, turning occasionally, until softened.

Increase the heat to high and cook for an additional 2 minutes, until the apples are starting to caramelize. Add the Calvados or other apple brandy and carefully flambé, swirling the skillet gently until the flames are gone.

Divide the apples between 2 bowls and pour the juices from the pan over them. Top each portion with a spoonful of crème fraîche or Greek yogurt and a pinch of cinnamon and serve immediately.

For apple & cinnamon French toast, beat 1 egg with 3 tablespoons milk, 1 tablespoon granulated sugar, and ½ teaspoon ground cinnamon. Add 2 slices of brioche and thoroughly coat both sides in the egg mixture. Melt 1 tablespoon unsalted butter in a large skillet and cook the bread for 2–3 minutes each side, until browned. Meanwhile, gently warm ¾ cup prepared applesauce in a small saucepan until it is hot. Serve the French toast topped with the warmed apple and scoops of vanilla ice cream.

chocolate banana-caramel pies

Serves **4**
Preparation time **5 minutes**

6 **chocolate-coated graham crackers** or **cookies**, coarsely crushed
1⅔ cups can dulce de leche **(caramel sauce)**
2 **bananas**, sliced
⅔ cup **whipped cream**
2 oz **semisweet chocolate**, shaved or grated

Divide the crushed crackers or cookies among 4 tall glasses. Spoon the dulce de leche over them and sprinkle the banana slices on top.

Top each portion with a spoonful of cream and decorate with the chocolate. Serve immediately.

For chocolate caramel sundaes, place 2 scoops of vanilla ice cream in each of 4 tall glasses. Melt 4 oz milk chocolate in a heatproof bowl set over a saucepan of gently simmering water, then mix in ¾ cup dulce de leche (caramel sauce). Spoon the chocolate caramel over the ice cream, then sprinkle with a handful of chopped toasted hazelnuts and 1 sliced banana. Serve immediately.

raspberry ice cream

Serves **4**
Preparation time **8 minutes**

1⅔ cups **frozen raspberries**
1 tablespoon **raspberry
   liqueur** or **lemon juice**
1 cup **mascarpone cheese**
2 tablespoons **confectioners'
   sugar**
thin cookies, to serve
   (optional)

Place the frozen raspberries in a food processor with the raspberry liqueur or lemon juice and blend until coarsely chopped.

Add the mascarpone and confectioners' sugar and blend until smooth. Serve immediately with thin cookies, if desired.

For raspberry & choc-chip ice cream sandwiches,
make the ice cream as above. Place a scoop of ice cream on each of 4 chocolate chip cookies and place another cookie on top of each to make sandwiches. Roll the edges of the sandwiches in ½ cup chopped pistachio nuts and serve immediately.

coffee desserts

Serves **6**
Preparation time **10 minutes**

4 teaspoons **instant
  espresso powder**
2 tablespoons **boiling water**
1 cup **mascarpone cheese**
3 tablespoons **confectioners'
  sugar**
1 cup **heavy whipping cream**
unsweetened cocoa powder,
  for dusting
6 **chocolate-covered coffee
  beans**, to decorate
cantucci or **amaretti cookies**,
  to serve

Place the espresso powder in a heatproof bowl with the boiling water, stir to dissolve, and let cool slightly.

Place the mascarpone and confectioners' sugar in a bowl and add the coffee. Beat, using a handheld electric mixer, until smooth.

Whip the cream with a handheld electric mixer until it forms soft peaks, then gently fold two-thirds of the cream into the coffee mixture. Divide the mixture among 6 espresso cups or small glasses, then top with the remaining cream.

Dust each portion with cocoa powder and decorate with a coffee bean. Serve immediately with the cookies.

For cappuccino meringues, make the coffee cream as above and use to fill 6 prepared meringue nests. Top with the remaining cream, then drizzle with a little melted semisweet chocolate to serve.

banana & chocolate ice pops

Serves **6**
Preparation time **7 minutes**
Cooking time **3 minutes**

4 oz **semisweet chocolate**,
  broken into small pieces
2 **bananas**
sugar strands or **sprinkles**,
  to decorate

Line a baking sheet with nonstick parchment paper and place in the freezer.

Melt the chocolate in a heatproof bowl set over a saucepan of gently simmering water, then let cool slightly.

Cut each banana into 3, then insert an ice cream stick into the end of each piece. Dip them, one at a time, into the melted chocolate to completely cover, using a spoon if necessary. Tap off the excess chocolate.

Sprinkle the ice pops with the sugar strands or sprinkles, place on the baking sheet, and return to the freezer for 3–4 minutes to set.

For waffles with banana & chocolate, lightly toast 6 waffles and divide among 6 bowls. Slice 6 bananas and arrange over the top of the waffles. Pour 1 ¼ cups warmed, prepared good-quality chocolate sauce over the banans and sprinkle with ¼ cup chopped hazelnuts. Serve immediately with vanilla ice cream.

muffin trifle with boozy berries

Serves **4**
Preparation time **10 minutes**

4 cups **mixed berries**, such
  as strawberries, raspberries,
  blueberries, and red currants,
  plus extra to decorate
3 tablespoons **crème de
  cerises** or **cherry brandy**
1 tablespoon **maple syrup**
2 large **blueberry muffins**,
  sliced
⅔ cup **heavy cream**

Put the fruit in a bowl with the cherry liqueur or brandy
and maple syrup and crush the berries with the back of
a fork until well combined.

Arrange the sliced muffins in the bottom of a glass dish
and spoon the fruit on top.

Whip the cream with a handheld electric mixer until it
forms soft peaks and spoon on top of the fruit. Decorate
with a few extra berries before serving.

For black forest trifle, slice 1 chocolate jelly roll and
arrange the slices in the bottom of a glass dish. Mix
1 (15 oz) can pitted black cherries, drained, with
3 tablespoons cherry brandy and 1 tablespoon maple
syrup and spoon into the bowl. Whip the cream as
above, adding the seeds scraped from a vanilla pod or
1 teaspoon vanilla extract, and arrange on top of the
cherries. Grate a little semisweet chocolate over the
trifle before serving.

chocolate & wasabi cheesecakes

Serves **4**
Preparation time **6 minutes**
Cooking time **3 minutes**

4 oz **white chocolate**, broken
  into small pieces, plus extra
  to decorate
4 **chocolate-coated graham
  crackers** or **cookies**,
  crushed
⅔ cup **soft cream cheese**
½ cup **heavy cream**
1–2 teaspoons **wasabi paste**
  or **hot English mustard**

Melt the chocolate in a heatproof bowl set over a
saucepan of gently simmering water, then let cool
slightly. Divide the crushed cracker or cookies among
4 glasses.

Whip the cream cheese and cream with a handheld
electric mixer for about 2 minutes, until the beaters
leave a trail, then stir in the melted chocolate and
wasabi paste or mustard to taste.

Spoon the mixture into the glasses and decorate
with grated chocolate. Serve immediately or chill
until ready to serve.

For mixed berries with white chocolate & mint,
place 5 oz white chocolate, broken into small pieces,
in a small saucepan with ½ cup heavy cream and
1 teaspoon peppermint extract. Stir over low heat
until the chocolate has melted. Divide 4 cups frozen
mixed berries, such as strawberries, raspberries, and
blueberries, among 4 bowls, pour the hot sauce over
the berries, and serve immediately.

orange & ginger brandy snaps

Serves **4**

Preparation time **10 minutes**

1 small **orange**

1 cup **heavy cream**

1 piece of **preserved ginger**, finely chopped, plus 1 tablespoon **syrup** from the jar

4 **prepared brandy snap baskets**

Grate the rind from half the orange, using a fine grater, and set aside, then remove the skin and pith. Divide the orange into segments by cutting between the membranes, working over a bowl to catch the juice.

Whip the cream and orange rind with a handheld electric mixer until it forms soft peaks, then add 2 tablespoons of the orange juice and the ginger syrup. Stir in the chopped ginger.

Divide the cream mixture among the brandy snap baskets, then top with the orange segments. Serve immediately.

For orange & ginger salad, slice the tops and bottoms off 4 oranges, then remove the skin and pith. Cut each orange into 6 slices, reserving the juice. Finely chop 2 pieces of preserved ginger. Place the reserved orange juice, the chopped ginger, and 2 tablespoons of ginger syrup from the jar in a bowl and mix together. Arrange the orange slices on a large plate and drizzle with the syrup. Sprinkle with a few mint leaves before serving.

chocolate mint mascarpone tart

Serves **6–8**
Preparation time **6 minutes**
Cooking time **3 minutes**

8 oz **semisweet chocolate
with mint crisp**, broken into
small pieces
⅔ cup **mascarpone cheese**
½ cup **heavy cream**
1 (8–9 inch) **prepared
pie crust**

To serve
crème fraîche or
whipped cream
unsweetened cocoa powder
mint leaves, to decorate

Melt the chocolate in a heatproof bowl set over a saucepan of gently simmering water, then let cool slightly.

Whip the mascarpone and cream with a handheld electric mixer until smooth and thickened. Stir in the melted chocolate until well combined, then spoon into the pie crust.

Serve in slices with spoonfuls of crème fraîche or whipped cream, a dusting of cocoa, and decorated with mint leaves.

For chocolate & chile fondue, place 8 oz chile-flavored semisweet chocolate, broken into small pieces, in a heatproof bowl with 1 ¼ cups heavy cream and 2 tablespoons unsalted butter. Heat gently for 5–7 minutes, stirring occasionally, until the mixture is smooth and glossy. Transfer to a fondue pot or warmed bowl and serve immediately with marshmallows and a selection of fruit, such as bananas and strawberries, for dipping.

raspberry & rose water meringues

Serves **4**
Preparation time **10 minutes**

¾ cup **raspberries**
1 tablespoon **confectioners' sugar**
½ cup **heavy cream**
1 teaspoon **rose water**
16 **prepared mini meringues**
¼ cup **raspberry coulis** or **raspberry sauce**

Place the raspberries in a small bowl with the confectioners' sugar and crush lightly with the back of a fork.

Whip the cream and rose water with a handheld electric mixer until it forms soft peaks, then gently fold in the crushed raspberries.

Spread some raspberry cream on the flat surface of a meringue, then sandwich together with another meringue. Repeat with the remaining meringues and cream. Serve the meringues with the raspberry coulis.

For raspberry & crushed meringues, lightly crush 4 prepared meringue nests. Whip ⅔ cup heavy cream with a handheld electric mixer until it forms soft peaks. Fold in ⅔ cup Greek yogurt, 1 cup raspberries, 3 tablespoons raspberry coulis or raspberry sauce, and the crushed meringues. Divide among 4 glasses and decorate with a few extra raspberries.

blackberry pancakes

Serves **2**
Preparation time **2 minutes**
Cooking time **8 minutes**

1 cup **blackberries**
1 tablespoon **lemon juice**
3 tablespoons **granulated
  sugar**
6 **prepared pancakes**
  or **waffles**
maple syrup, to serve

Place the blackberries, lemon juice, and sugar in a small saucepan. Cook over medium heat for 4–5 minutes, stirring occasionally, until softened. Let cool slightly.

Meanwhile, preheat a ridged grill pan and cook the pancakes for 1 minute on each side, until heated through.

Divide the pancakes between 2 serving plates and pour the blackberry sauce over them. Drizzle with a little maple syrup and serve immediately.

For pancakes with lemon mascarpone, mix
½ cup mascarpone cheese with 2 tablespoons lemon curd. Grill the pancakes as above and serve the warm pancakes with a spoonful of lemon mascarpone and a handful of fresh raspberries.

caipirinha lime syllabub

Serves **4**
Preparation time **10 minutes**

¼ cup **granulated sugar**
finely grated rind and juice
 of 2 **limes**
1 cup **heavy cream**
¼ cup **cachaça** or **white rum**
pared lime rind, to decorate
shortbread cookies, to serve

Place the sugar, finely grated lime rind, and lime juice in a small bowl and stir to dissolve the sugar.

Whip the cream with a handheld electric mixer until it forms soft peaks. Slowly beat in the cachaça or rum, then add the lime mixture. Beat until thick and fluffy, then spoon into 4 glasses. Decorate with lime rind and serve with shortbread cookies.

For limoncello zabaglione, place 4 egg yolks and ¼ cup granulated sugar in a large heatproof bowl and beat with a handheld electric mixer for 2 minutes, until the mixture is pale and thick. Gradually beat in ¼ cup limoncello, a tablespoon at a time. Place the bowl over a saucepan of gently simmering water and beat for 5–7 minutes, until thick and the beaters leave a trail on the surface. Pour into 4 glasses and serve immediately with amaretti cookies.

mango & passion fruit yogurt

Serves **4**
Preparation time **10 minutes**

1 large **mango**, peeled, pitted,
  and chopped
3 cups **plain yogurt**
1–2 tablespoons **agave
  nectar**
1 **vanilla bean**, split in half
  lengthwise, or 1 teaspoon
  vanilla extract
4 **passion fruit**, halved
butter cookies, to serve

Place the mango in a food processor and blend to
a puree. Place the yogurt in a large bowl and add the
agave nectar to taste. Scape in the seeds from the
vanilla bean or add the lemon extract and beat together
until well combined.

Gently fold the mango puree into the yogurt mixture
and divide among 4 glasses. Scoop the seeds from
the passion fruit over the mango yogurt and serve
immediately with cookies.

For blueberry & almond yogurt, puree 2 cups
blueberries as above and fold into the yogurt with
the agave nectar, according to taste, and 1 teaspoon
almond extract. Spoon into tall glasses and sprinkle
with toasted almonds, to serve.

index

234

acknowledgments

Executive editor: Eleanor Maxfield
Art direction and design: Penny Stock
Photography: William Shaw
Home economy: Denise Smart
Styling: Kim Sullivan
Assistant production manager: Caroline Alberti

Photography copyright © Octopus Publishing Group
Limited/William Shaw, except the following: copyright ©
Octopus Publishing Group/Stephen Conroy 9, 13, 29,
219; Will Heap 14, 17, 87, 95, 101, 119, 169, 183;
William Lingwood 37, 43, 171; David Munns 151, 165;
Lis Parsons 19, 49, 111, 121, 137, 145, 161, 191;
William Reavell 133